French
Verb
HANDBOOK

Kate Dobson

French Verb Handbook

The Author:

Kate Dobson is an experienced teacher at primary school, high school and adult level.

The Series Editor:

Christopher Wightwick is a former UK representative on the Council of Europe Modern Languages Project and principal Inspector of Modern Languages for England.

Other titles in the Berlitz Language Handbook Series:

French Grammar Handbook	French Vocabulary Handbook ('94)
German Grammar Handbook	German Vocabulary Handbook ('94)
Spanish Grammar Handbook	Spanish Vocabulary Handbook ('94)
German Verb Handbook	
Spanish Verb Handbook	

Published by Berlitz Publishing Co., Ltd.,
Peterley Road, Oxford OX4 2TX, U.K.

1st printing 1993

Printed in the U.S.A.

CONTENTS

How to use this Handbook

This handbook aims to provide a full description of the French verb system for all learners and users of the French language. It provides the following information:

• a chapter on the verb system;
• the conjugation in full of sixty-one common verbs, grouped to show the common patterns underlying the system;
• a full subject index;
• a verb index containing over 2,300 verbs with their English meanings.

An important feature of the handbook is that examples, showing many of the verbs in use, are given in the model verb pages.

VERBS IN FRENCH: their functions and uses

This section describes the functions of verbs in general. Information is given on word order, the use of tenses, the way verbs govern different cases and prepositions and the way they are formed.

MODEL FRENCH VERBS

This section gives the conjugation in full of every tense of a verb. The reflexive verb form is also illustrated. Fifty-six common verbs are then set out as models.

A selection of verbs which follow the same pattern as each individual verb is listed underneath. Examples are then provided of these verbs in use, to illustrate different tenses and a wide range of different meanings and idiomatic constructions.

THE SUBJECT INDEX

The subject index gives paragraph references for all the main grammatical terms used.

THE VERB INDEX

For each verb, information is given on whether it is transitive or intransitive, the auxiliary it takes in the past tenses, the prepositions which it governs and its English meaning. Common secondary meanings are illustrated in a brief phrase. The most important and up-to-date forms of verbs are listed.

HOW TO FIND THE INFORMATION YOU WANT

If you want to check on the form, meaning or use of a verb, first look it up in the index. This gives a range of information:

• Any preposition which normally follows the verb.
• Whether the verb is transitive, intransitive, reflexive or impersonal, and whether it takes the auxiliary **être** in the compound past tenses. If no auxiliary is shown, the verb takes **avoir**.
• The English meaning of the verb. Only the basic meaning is shown for most verbs.
• A number indicating on which model verb page or pages you will find further information about the verb or others like it.
• A short phrase or sentence following some verbs, giving important subsidiary meanings.

If you want further information on the form or use of the verb, turn to the model verb reference given. On these pages you will find:

• the full conjugation of the present, perfect, imperfect and simple past of each model verb;
• the first person singular form of other tenses;
• a list of other verbs following the same pattern;
• notes indicating any exceptions to this pattern;
• short dialogues and sentences illustrating some of the different tenses and usages of these verbs.

If you want to know the full form of other tenses you should note that they are always regular. They can easily be checked by looking up the full tense of the relevant verb:

• **marcher** [➤1] a regular **-er** verb taking **avoir**;
• **tomber** [➤2] a regular **-er** verb taking **être**;
• **se laver** [➤3] a regular reflexive **-er** verb;
• **finir** [➤16] a regular **-ir** verb;
• **vendre** [➤28] a regular **-re** verb.

For further information on how the verb system works, refer to Verbs in French: their functions and uses.

A

VERBS IN FRENCH:
THEIR FUNCTIONS AND USES

1   *What do verbs do?*

2   *What verbs govern*

3   *Attitudes to action: modal verbs*

4   *Verb forms not related to time*

5   *What else do French verbs do*

For a full treatment of this topic, see Berlitz *French Grammar Handbook.*

What do verbs do?

1a Full verbs

'Full' verbs in French do the same job as in English: that is, they communicate the action, or feeling, state or changing state of the subject. Their position in the sentence is similar to English word order:

Subject (noun or pronoun) – verb – rest of sentence

Mon frère a bu tout le champagne.	My brother has drunk all the champagne.
Il aime le vin rouge aussi.	He likes red wine too.
Maintenant il a la gueule de bois.	Now he has got a hangover.

1b Auxiliary verbs

Some verbs have a use as 'auxiliary' verbs. In French, **avoir** 'to have' and **être** 'to be' are the auxiliary verbs, which means they are used in their various simple tenses, with the past participle of other verbs, in the formation of all the compound tenses. (Compare the use of the verb 'to have' in English.)

• *avoir*:

j'ai mangé	I have eaten
j'avais mangé	I had eaten
j'aurais mangé	I would have eaten

• *être*:

je suis tombé	I have fallen over
j'étais tombé	I had fallen
je serais tombé	I should have fallen

What verbs govern

All sentences consist of a subject, and the rest of the sentence, known as the 'predicate'. The predicate may be just a verb, or a verb plus more information.

2a   Subject + verb + complement

Some verbs just link the subject to the rest of the information, which is known as the 'complement'. The verb **être** 'to be' is frequently used in this way.

Il est pharmacien.	He is a pharmacist.
Elle a été actrice.	She was an actress.

2b   Verbs which need no further completion

Le facteur arrive.	The mailman's/postman's arriving.

In this sentence the verb is complete in itself. Other information could be added, such as **maintenant** 'now', or **à vélo** 'by bike'. The verb would nevertheless be complete. This type of verb is called 'intransitive'; verbs which are only intransitive in use are marked 'intr' in the Index of this handbook.

2c   Verbs which have an object

Il regarde les adresses sur les lettres.	He's looking at the addresses on the letters.

Here, the verb requires a noun phrase to complete the sense, i.e. the addresses. The 'direct object' of the verb is the item(s) or person(s) directly affected by the action. **Regarder** is a verb needing a direct object, and is called 'transitive'. Such verbs are marked 'tr' in the Index.

A considerable number of verbs can be either transitive or intransitive – these are marked 'tr/intr' (e.g. **changer**).

2d   *Verb + preposition + object*

French verbs do not always have the same relationship with the rest of the sentence as their English counterparts. Verbs which are transitive in English may need a preposition before the object in French; and the converse is true.

Je me suis emparé *de* la bouteille, et j'ai téléphoné *au* docteur.	I grabbed the bottle and phoned the doctor.
J'ai attendu le docteur une demi heure.	I waited half an hour for the doctor

A list of verbs like **attendre** would include:

chercher	to look for	**habiter**	to live in/at
demander	to ask for	**regarder**	to look at
écouter	to listen to		

Here it is the English which adds the preposition. When a verb requires a preposition in either language, the preposition is given in the Index. A full list of these verbs may be found in the *Grammar Handbook*, ➤8e.

2e   *Verbs which have two objects – direct and indirect*
(i)

Le facteur a donné deux lettres à mon patron.	The postman gave two letters to my boss.

Here the direct object of the verb consists of the two letters, given to the indirect object, the boss.

(ii)   Sometimes in English we omit the word 'to' in such sentences:

He gave the boss the letters.

With French nouns, the direct plus indirect object sentence can only be expressed as shown above; the indirect object always follows **à**. When pronouns are involved the word order makes the meaning clear.

Il m'a offert des fleurs.	He gave me some flowers (*as a gift*).
Il me les a offertes pour mon anniversaire.	He gave them to me for my birthday.

– Où est ton stylo?	– Where's your pen?
– **Je le lui ai donné.**	– I gave it to her.

2f Reflexive verbs

(i) Some verbs express an action which is turned back on the subject: the object is the same person as the subject.

Je me pèse une fois par semaine.	I weigh myself once a week.

(ii) Sometimes people are doing the action not to themselves but to each other, in which case the subject is invariably plural.

Ils s'aiment à la folie.	They love each other madly.

(iii) In many cases the French reference to self or each other is not expressed in English.

Je m'habille dans ma chambre.	I get dressed in my room.
Il se fatigue vite.	He gets tired quickly.

(iv) With some verbs the reflexive idea has largely disappeared, but the grammatical form still applies.

Je me suis aperçu de son indifference.	I noticed his indifference.

2g Verbs governing verbs

(i) *Combining verbs*

More complex sentences are made in both French and English combining two verbs. The combinations are not always parallel.

J'aime aller en France.	I like to go to France *or* I like going to France.
Je dois partir demain.	I must leave tomorrow.

Je t'invite à m'accompagner.	I invite you to come with me.
J'ai oublié d'acheter des chèques de voyage.	I've forgotten to buy some travellers' checks/cheques.

Each of these complex sentences in French follows one of two possible patterns:
• verb + infinitive;
• verb + preposition + infinitive.

The infinitive is the part of the verb which has the meaning 'to do', 'to play' etc [➤4a].

The commonest prepositions used in the structure are **à** and **de**, and the student needs to check which verb follows which pattern. The Index and larger dictionaries give this information. (➤Berlitz *French Grammar Handbook*, 8f.)

(ii) It should be noted that the French present participle (**jouant**, **cherchant**) cannot be used here, even though in English the form ending in -ing may be possible.

J'aime chanter.	I like singing/I like to sing.
Je préfère nager.	I prefer swimming/I prefer to swim.

(A) Some of the verbs followed immediately by an infinitive are the modal verbs [➤3] and:

souhaiter	to wish to
espérer	to hope to
monter	to go up
aller	to go/to be going to
entendre	to hear (someone doing something)
voir	to see (someone doing something)
faire	to have/get something done

Je souhaite faire sa connaissance.	I really hope to meet him.
On espère vous voir au concert.	We hope to see you at the concert.
Nous allons partir en vacances.	We're going to go on vacation.
On les entend crier.	You can hear them shouting.
Je l'ai vu venir.	I saw him coming.
Je fais réparer la télé.	I'm getting the TV repaired.
Je fais construire une maison.	I'm having a house built.

(B) Verbs requiring **à** before an infinitive include

apprendre à	to learn to
commencer à	to begin to
demander à	to ask to
hésiter à	to hesitate to
réussir à	to succeed in (doing)
renoncer à	to give up (doing)

J'apprends à faire de la planche à voile.	I'm learning windsurfing.
Il a hésité à parler au patron.	He hesitated to speak to the boss.
On a réussi à réparer le voiture.	We managed to repair the car.

(C) Verbs requiring **de** before an infinitive include

accuser de	to accuse (*someone of doing*)
demander à X de	to ask someone to do
essayer de	to try to
oublier de	to forget to
permettre de	to allow to

J'ai oublié de chercher mon appareil.	I forgot to fetch my camera.
Elle m'a accusé de tricher.	She accused me of cheating.
On va essayer de finir avant cinq heures.	We're going to try and finish by five o'clock.

This is a much bigger group than the other two, and most verbs come into this category.

Attitudes to action: modal verbs

3a   Modal verbs are not usually complete in meaning in themselves: they create a mood for, or an attitude towards the verb which follows. The following verb must be in the infinitive in French.

Je dois partir.	I must leave.
Pouvez-vous appeler un taxi?	Can you call a taxi?
Je voudrais arriver chez moi avant minuit.	I'd like to get home by midnight.

3b   The modal verbs in French are:

devoir	to have to
falloir	to be necessary (only exists in the third person singular form as an impersonal verb)
pouvoir	to be able
savoir	to know how to
vouloir	to want to

More examples of their use are given on the corresponding verb pages.

Note   **Devoir**, **savoir** and **vouloir** also have independent use, as well as modal function. They mean 'to owe', 'to know' and 'to want' respectively.

Verb forms not related to time

4a *The infinitive*

(i)   This is the name part of the verb, determining its entry in the dictionary, used as a noun, as a verb in the various structures outlined above, and after certain prepositions.

Infinitives in French can be identified by the endings **-er**, **-ir**, **-re** and **-oir**. *All infinitives have one of these endings, but the endings are not exclusive to verbs.*

(ii)   Infinitives as nouns:

le rire	laughter	**le devoir**	duty
le déjeuner	lunch	**le souvenir**	memory, souvenir

Some infinitives appear as nouns, but not all can be used this way; it is advisable to check in a dictionary.

Note   Sometimes an infinitive may appear as the subject of the verb:

Travailler **ici me rend malade!**   *Working* here makes me ill!

(iii)   Useful expressions which can be used for any person, in combination with any tense:

pour arriver	in order to arrive	**avant de partir**	before leaving
afin d'arriver	in order to arrive	**sans attendre**	without waiting

4b *Present participle*

(i)   The present participle can be formed from the **nous** form of the present tense, by replacing the **-ons** with **-ant**. It means 'doing' 'singing', 'eating', etc.

(ii)   Its uses are as an adjective, occasionally as noun, and in the very useful structure: **en + present participle** 'by/while/in/on doing'. This can be used for any person, and with any tense, without alteration.

Elle est passée nous voir en rentrant chez elle.	She popped in to see us on the way home. (*Literally 'while going home'*)

[➤also 4c(iv) below]

Note: In French 'before doing' and 'without doing' both require the *infinitive,* not the present participle.

(iii) Note also: No progressive/continuous present tense can be constructed using this participle.

Je travaille.	I am working.

4c *Past participle*

(i) Past participles of regular verbs are formed by adding **-é** (**-er** erbs), **-i** (**-ir** verbs) or **-u** (**-re** verbs) to the stem of the infinitive. The stem is formed by removing **-er**, **-ir** or **-re**. Irregular verbs may not follow this pattern, and many past participles need to be learnt individually, e.g. **boire – bu**; **écrire – écrit**; **faire – fait**; **lire – lu**.

(ii) The past participle is used:

- as the second item in all the compound past tenses.
- with any tense of **être** to create the passive form, e.g. **Il a été cassé** (It has been broken);
- as in English as an adjective, when it follows the noun, e.g. **la voiture volée** (the stolen car).

(iii) Note also the French for 'after doing', which uses a past infinitive made with **avoir** or **être** + the past participle.

Après avoir acheté les timbres, il est parti.	After buying the stamps, he left.
Après être arrivés, ils ont loué une voiture.	After arriving, they hired a car.

(iv) There also exists the equivalent of English 'having done', combining both participles:

Ayant acheté les timbres ...   Having bought the stamps ...

(v)   In literary contexts the past participle of certain verbs – those conjugated with **être** in compound tenses – may be used alone in an absolute construction:

Une fois arrivé à Paris, il a cherché un hôtel.   Having arrived in Paris, he looked for a hotel.

For rules governing the agreements of the past participle in compound tenses ➤Berlitz *French Grammar Handbook.*

What else do French verbs do?

The various tenses in common use given in the verb tables are listed below, with their characteristic endings, and the meanings.

For a full study of French tenses ➤Berlitz *French Grammar Handbook*, 11.

5a   *Pronouns*

The verb tables are presented with the personal subject pronouns which are used in French very much as in English.

- **je** (**j'** before vowel or ordinary **h**) – 'I';
- **tu** – 'you' (singular). This is the form of address for family members, close friends, small children and pets;
- **il** – 'he'; also 'it', when the name of a thing is masculine;
- **elle** – 'she'; also 'it', when the name of a thing is feminine;
- **on** – '. . .'. This is presented in this book as a separate entry because of its great importance in the French language, particularly the spoken language. It is commonly used for 'we' (colloquially, alongside **nous**, because the shorter verb forms are quicker), 'you' (generally), 'they', 'everyone', 'people', 'someone', and occasionally 'one';
- **nous** – 'we';
- **vous** – 'you'. Used as the normal form of address to a single individual who is not a close friend or relative and as the plural 'you' when talking to a group of people;
- **ils** – 'they', referring to people and things which are either all masculine or a mixture of masculine and feminine;
- **elles** – 'they', referring to people and things which are all feminine.

5b   *Pronunciation*

These few pointers may prove useful when studying verbs.

(i)   *Pronounciation of pronouns*

The **-s** which is normally silent at the end of pronouns **nous**, **vous**, **ils** and **elles** must always be pronounced as **z** if the verb begins with a vowel or **h**. This is called 'liaison'.

Ils aiment les films italiens.	They like Italian films.
Nous arrivons à midi.	We are arriving at midday.
Ils habitent à Milan.	They live in Milan.

Note that words beginning with aspirate **h**, marked with an asterisk in the index and in dictionaries, require no liaison.

(ii) *Pronounciation of verb endings*

• **-er**, the ending of very many infinitives, is pronounced like **é**;
• **-ant**, the ending of the present participle, is pronounced without the **-t** as the single nasal vowel of the word **en**;
• **-e**, **-es**, **-s**, **-x**, **-t** endings on any verbs are silent;
• **-ons**, the ending for **nous** (first person plural), is pronounced like the end of **bon**, the **-s** being silent;
• **-ez**, the ending for **vous** (second person plural), is pronounced like **é**;
• **-ent**, the ending for third person plural verbs, is always silent;
• **ont** has the same pronunciation as **-ons**;
• **-ais**, **-ait**, **-aient** endings of the imperfect tense are pronounced as the **-e-** in the English word 'let'.

5c *French verb forms given in this book*

(i) *Infinitive* ➤4a
Present participle ➤4b
Past participle ➤4c

(ii) *Imperative*

(A) Imperatives are given in the verb tables. They are the expressions used for requests and commands. They are normally the **tu**, **nous** and **vous** present tense forms *without the subject pronoun* but, except before **y** and **en**, **-er** verbs drop the final **-s** of the **tu** form.

va-t'en	go away!	but:
vas-y	go to it!	

(B) As the imperative form can sound rather abrupt, it is common to find requests phrased:

Veux-tu/Voulez-vous ouvrir la porte?	Will you open the door?

or

Tu pourrais/vous pourriez ouvrir la porte?	Could you open the door?

(C) When instructions are given for a process, as in recipes, it is also common to find the infinitive used as the imperative:

Délayer le beurre et le sucre.	Cream the butter and sugar.
Ajouter 500 grammes de farine.	Add 500 grams of flour.

(iii) *Tenses of the indicative*

The indicative tenses are the ordinary verbs which make statements about what is happening, has happened, or will happen. However, they do not only communicate the timing of the action; they may also give the speaker's or writer's perspective on the event.

Use of tenses in French is not directly equivalent to English. The following examples, taken from the verb **parler** (to speak), make this clear.

(A) Simple tenses (where the verb is a single word)

• Present tense: **je parle**
There are three 'regular' patterns for the present tense of verbs whose infinitives end in **-er**, **-ir** and **-re**. All these and the variants and exceptions are set out in the model verb pages.

The French present tense covers the usages of all three English versions: 'I speak', 'I am speaking', 'I do speak'. In ournalistic accounts it is also very common to find the present tense used to recount the action of the story more vividly than if a past tense were used. This is called the 'historic present'.

• Imperfect tense: **je parlais**
This tense refers to incomplete or continuing action in the past. It can mean: 'I spoke', 'I was speaking', 'I used to speak' or 'I would speak' (often).

With the exception of **être (j'étais)**, all verbs form the imperfect tense using the **nous** form stem from the present tense. Simply remove the **-ons** ending of the present and add the endings:

(je) -ais	(il/elle/on) -ait	(vous) -iez
(tu) -ais	(nous) -ions	(ils) -aient

• Simple past: **je parlai**
This tense, used mainly in written narrative to tell the events of the story, means 'spoke'. In regular verbs the stem is that of the infinitive minus **-er/-ir/-re**. The endings are:

-ai, -as, -a, -âmes, -âtes, -èrent (**-er** verbs)
-is, -is, -it, -îmes, -îtes, -irent (**-ir** and **-re** verbs)

There are a number of irregular verbs with the endings:

-us, -us, -ut, -ûmes, -ûtes, -urent

(➤ Model Verb Pages)

• Future: **je parlerai**
The simple future is the equivalent of English 'shall speak/will speak'. The endings for the future are derived from the present tense of **avoir**:

-ai, -as, -a, -ons, -ez, -ont

These are added to a stem which in most verbs is the whole infinitive (**-er** or **-ir** verbs) or the infinitive minus the final **-e** (**-re** verbs). There are a number of exceptions to this simple rule; these need to be learned individually.

• Conditional: **je parlerais**
This tense means 'would speak'. The stem is that of the future tense, and the endings are those of the imperfect tense:

-ais, -ais, -ait, -ions, -iez, -aient

(B) Compound tenses – the verb consists of two words or more

• Perfect tense: **j'ai parlé**
This is the tense for completed action in the past, in speech and in writing, meaning 'I spoke', 'I did speak' or 'I have spoken'. It is formed from the present tense of **avoir** or **être** and the past participle of the verb. Most verbs use **avoir** as the auxiliary. A small number of very common verbs and *all* reflexive verbs use **être**.

• Past perfect or pluperfect: **j'avais parlé**
This tense means 'had spoken'. It is formed from the imperfect of **avoir** or **être** and the past participle.

• Past anterior: **j'eus parlé**
This tense is found in written narrative where the main action is conveyed in the simple past. It has the meaning 'had spoken'. It occurs after conjunctions of time (**quand**, **dès que**, **aussitôt que**) and is formed with the simple past of **avoir** or **être** and the past participle.

• Future perfect: **j'aurai parlé**
This tense means 'will have spoken'. It is formed from the future tense of **avoir** or **être** and the past participle. It expresses probability and must also be used after conjunctions of time (**quand**, **dès que**, **aussitôt que**) referring to the future.

• Conditional perfect: **j'aurais parlé**
The meaning of this tense is 'would have spoken'. It is formed from the conditional tense of **avoir** or **être** and the past participle.

(iv) Tenses of the subjunctive

The subjunctive is used in French in subordinate clauses after conjunctions such as **quoique** (although), **pourvu que** (provided that), **afin que** (in order to), and after verbs of wishing, fearing, doubting and other emotions. It also occurs occasionally as a main verb to express a formalized wish: **Vive la France!**

The present and perfect tenses are the ones most frequently used, and are in practice the main tenses in colloquial use. The imperfect subjunctive may occur occasionally in speech in its shorter forms; this and the pluperfect subjunctive are more likely to be found in literary texts. Giving an English equivalent of each tense is not practical, as often structures do not correspond in the two languages.

• Present tense: **que je parle**
Apart from a few irregular verbs, the present subjunctive is formed from the third person plural of the present indicative. For the singular and the third person plural, simply delete the **-ent** ending and add the endings:

-e, -es, -e, -ent
The **nous** and **vous** forms are the same as in the imperfect indicative:

-ions, -iez
These endings also apply to irregular verbs, but the stem changes. The verbs which are irregular in the present subjective are:

avoir – que j'aie	que nous *ayons*
être – que je sois	que nous *soyons*
aller – que j'aille	que nous allions
faire – que je fasse	que nous *fassions*
falloir – qu' il faille	
pouvoir – que je puisse	que nous *puissions*
savoir – que je sache	que nous *sachions*
valoir – que je vaille	que nous valions
vouloir – que je veuille	que nous voulions

(The *italics* show **nous** and **vous** forms which are also irregular.)

Je veux que tu *ailles* chez Michel.	I want you to go to Michel's.
Je veux bien lui parler pourvu	I don't mind talking to him
qu'il *vienne* avant dix heures.	provided he comes before ten.

- Perfect tense: **que j'aie parlé**
  This is formed from the present subjunctive of **avoir** or **être**
  plus the past participle.

| C'est dommage que tu *aies* | It's a pity *you've lost* your purse. |
| *perdu* ton porte-monnaie. | |

- Imperfect tense: **que je parlasse**
  This tense is not often found except in the third person singular
  (**parlât**). It is replaced in conversation by the present subjunctive.

| J'ignorais qu'il *possédât* un | I didn't know *he had* a gun . . . |
| fusil . . . | |

- Pluperfect tense: **que j'eusse parlé**
  This is formed from the imperfect subjunctive of **avoir** or **être**
  and the past participle. It is not often found in speech.

| . . . et je fus indigné qu'il *eût* | . . . and I was annoyed that *he had* |
| *gardé* un si beau secret.* | *kept* such a fine secret to himself. |

* (Marcel Pagnol: *La Gloire de mon père*)

(v) *The passive*

When the action is done *to* the subject of the sentence, the
passive form may be needed. This is composed of the appro-
priate tense of **être** (to be) followed by the past participle.

| L'enfant a été blessé. | The child was hurt. |

The passive is as widely used in French as it is in English, but
sometimes the passive in English is replaced by **on**:

| Ici on parle anglais | English is spoken here |

or a reflexive verb:

Ce vin se trouve facilement en Bourgogne.	That wine is easily found in Burgundy.

5d   *Asking questions*

(i)   *'Do you like shellfish?'*

In French there are three possible ways of saying this:

(A) Aimes-tu les fruits de mer? (Verb and subject change places.)

(B) Est-ce que tu aimes les fruits de mer? (The formula **est-ce que** precedes the statement and makes it into a question.)

(C) Tu aimes les fruits de mer? (Same word order as a statement, but the voice tone rises at the end of the sentence, creating the question.)

(ii)   The same variations are possible when a question word, such as **quand?** (when?) or **où?** (where?), is involved.

(A) Où habitez-vous?

(B) Où est-ce que vous habitez?

(C) Vous habitez où?

Note that when the subject is a noun phrase, it is only possible to use (A) by adding a pronoun:

Les Borgia ont-*ils* empoisonné tous leurs ennemis?	Did the Borgias poison all their enemies?

As this is fairly formal, in conversation (B) or (C) are more usual for such longer, more complex questions.

5e   *Not, never, no more*

(i)   Making statements and questions negative in French involves using one of the expressions:

ne . . . pas	not
ne . . . plus	no more, no longer
ne . . . rien	nothing, not anything

ne . . . jamais	never, not ever
ne . . . personne	nobody, not anybody
ne . . . que	only, nothing but
ne . . . aucun (+ noun)	no, not any

Je *n'*aime *pas* les fruits de mer.	I don't like sea-food.
Vous *n'*avez *pas* d'allumettes?	Haven't you any matches?
Il *ne* fume *plus*.	He doesn't smoke any more.
Il *ne* boit *rien*.	He doesn't drink anything.
Elle *ne* m'écoute *jamais*.	She never listens to me.
Il *n'*y a *personne*.	There's no one (there).

(ii)   These negative expressions, as may be seen, are positioned around the verb. In compound tenses the negative expression is usually around the auxiliary verb.

Je *n'*ai *pas* trouvé mon sac.	I haven't found my bag.
Elle *n'*a *rien* bu.	She didn't drink anything.
Nous *n'*y sommes *jamais* allés.	We've never been there.

Except:

On *n'*a vu *personne*.	We didn't see anyone.
Il *n'*a apporté *que* trois bouteilles de vin.	He only bought three bottles of wine.
La police *n'*as trouvé *aucune* trace des voleurs.	The police found no trace of the thieves.

For a more comprehensive treatment ➤Berlitz *French Grammar Handbook.*

B
MODEL FRENCH VERBS

Index of verbs

Full conjugations

-ER verbs

-IR verbs

-RE verbs

-OIR verbs

Index of verbs

On the following pages are set out verb tables. Some verbs are given in full, others show the full forms of the Present, Perfect, Imperfect and Simple Past tenses only, giving the first person singular of the other tenses. These tenses then follow the patterns laid out in the full conjugation pages.

Full conjugations: *Number*

marcher	walk	1
tomber	fall	2
se laver	wash, get washed	3
avoir	have	4
être	be	5
être blessé	be wounded	6

(➤ also **finir** 16; **vendre** 28)

-er verbs:

parler	speak	7
aller	go	8
appeler	call	9
acheter	buy	10
céder	give way	11
employer	employ	12
manger	eat	13
placer	place	14
payer	pay	15

-ir verbs:

finir	finish	16
acquérir	acquire	17
cueillir	pick	18
courir	run	19
dormir	sleep	20
faillir	almost do	21
fuir	flee	22
mourir	die	23
ouvrir	open	24

Example of verb using **avoir** in compound tenses

IMPERATIVE
marché (tu)   marchez! (vous)   marchons! (nous)

PRESENT
je marche
tu marches
il/elle marche
on marche
nous marchons
vous marchez
ils/elles marchent

PERFECT
j'ai marché
tu as marché
il/elle a marché
on a marché
nous avons marché
vous avez marché
ils/elles ont marché

IMPERFECT
je marchais
tu marchais
il/elle marchait
on marchait
nous marchions
vous marchiez
ils/elles marchaient

SIMPLE PAST
je marchai
tu marchas
il/elle marcha
on marcha
nous marchâmes
vous marchâtes
ils/elles marchèrent

PAST PERFECT
j'avais marché
tu avais marché
il/elle avait marché
on avait marché
nous avions marché
vous aviez marché
ils/elles avaient marché

PAST ANTERIOR
j'eus marché
tu eus marché
il/elle eut marché
on eut marché
nous eûmes marché
vous eûtes marché
ils/elles eurent marché

PRESENT PARTICIPLE
marchant

PAST PARTICIPLE
marché

FUTURE
je marcherai
tu marcheras
il/elle marchera
on marchera
nous marcherons
vous marcherez
ils/elles marcheront

FUTURE PERFECT
j'aurai marché
tu auras marché
il/elle aura marché
on aura marché
nous aurons marché
vous aurez marché
ils/elles auront marché

CONDITIONAL
je marcherais
tu marcherais
il/elle marcherait
on marcherait
nous marcherions
vous marcheriez
ils/elles marcheraient

CONDITIONAL PERFECT
j'aurais marché
tu aurais marché
il/elle aurait marché
on aurait marché
nous aurions marché
vous auriez marché
ils/elles auraient marché

PRESENT SUBJUNCTIVE
que je marche
que tu marches
qu'il/elle marche
qu'on marche
que nous marchions
que vous marchiez
qu'ils/elles marchent

PERFECT SUBJUNCTIVE
que j'aie marché
que tu aies marché
qu'il/elle ait marché
qu'on ait marché
que nous ayons marché
que vous ayez marché
qu'ils/elles aient marché

IMPERFECT SUBJUNCTIVE
que je marchasse
que tu marchasses
qu'il/elle marchât
qu'on marchât
que nous marchassions
que vous marchassiez
qu'ils/elles marchassent

PLUPERFECT SUBJUNCTIVE
que j'eusse marché
que tu eusses marché
qu'il/elle eût marché
qu'on eût marché
que nous eussions marché
que vous eussiez marché
qu'ils/elles eussent marché

Notes 1) This example of a verb conjugated with **avoir** in compound tenses is given in full for reference.
2) **Marcher** is a regular **-er** verb; the majority of regular and irregular verbs use **avoir** as the auxiliary verb to form the compound tenses.

J'*ai* bien *travaillé* ce matin.	I'*ve worked* well this morning.
J'*ai gagné* le gros lot!	I'*ve won* the jackpot!
Les copains *ont proposé* d'aller à la plage.	The friends *suggested* going to the beach.
Nous *avons manqué* le train.	We *missed* the train.
Vous *avez retrouvé* votre portefeuille?	*Did* you *find* your wallet?
On *avait fini* de travailler avant midi.	We *had finished* working before midday.
Je *suppose* que tu n'*auras* pas *eu* le temps de lire les documents?	I *suppose* you won't *have had* time to read the documents?
Je suis désolé que vous n'ayez pas pu *assister* à notre mariage.	I'm so sorry you weren't able *to come* to our wedding.
J'*aurais invité* mes parents, mais ils sont en Australie.	I *would have invited* my parents, but they're in Australia.
On *aurait pris* un pot si on *avait eu* le temps.	We *would have had* a drink if we'*d had* time.

Example of verb using **être** in compound tenses

PRESENT PARTICIPLE

tombant

PAST PARTICIPLE

tombé

IMPERATIVE

tombe! (tu)   tombez! (vous)   tombons! (nous)

PRESENT

je tombe
tu tombes
il/elle tombe
on tombe
nous tombons
vous tombez
ils/elles tombent

PERFECT

je suis tombé/tombée
tu es tombé/tombée
il est tombé
elle est tombée
on est tombé
nous sommes tombés/tombées
vous êtes tombé/tombée/
  tombés/tombées
ils sont tombés
elles sont tombées

IMPERFECT

je tombais
tu tombais
il/elle tombait
on tombait
nous tombions
vous tombiez
ils/elles tombaient

SIMPLE PAST

je tombai
tu tombas
il/elle tomba
on tomba
nous tombâmes
vous tombâtes
ils/elles tombèrent

PAST PERFECT

j'étais tombé(-e)
tu étais tombé(-e)
il était tombé
elle était tombée
nous étions tombés(-es)
vous étiez tombé(-e/-s/-es)
ils étaient tombés
elles étaient tombées

PAST ANTERIOR

je fus tombé(-e)
tu fus tombé(-e)
il fut tombé
elle fut tombée
nous fûmes tombés(-es)
vous fûtes tombé(-e/-s/-es)
ils furent tombés
elles furent tombées

FUTURE

je tomberai
tu tomberas
il/elle tombera
on tombera
nous tomberons
vous tomberez
ils/elles tomberont

CONDITIONAL

je tomberais
tu tomberais
il/elle tomberait
on tomberait
nous tomberions
vous tomberiez
ils/elles tomberaient

PRESENT SUBJUNCTIVE

que je tombe
que tu tombes
qu'il/elle tombe
qu'on tombe
que nous tombions
que vous tombiez
qu'ils/elles tombent

IMPERFECT SUBJUNCTIVE

que je tombasse
que tu tombasses
qu'il/elle tombât
qu'on tombât
que nous tombassions
que vous tombassiez
qu'ils/elles tombassent

FUTURE PERFECT

je serai tombé(-e)
tu seras tombé(-e)
il sera tombé on sera tombé
elle sera tombée
nous serons tombés(-es)
vous serez tombé(-e/-s/-es)
ils seront tombés
elles seront tombées

CONDITIONAL PERFECT

je serais tombé(-e)
tu serais tombé(-e)
il serait tombé
elle serait tombée
on serait tombé
nous serions tombés(-es)
vous seriez tombé(-e/-s/-es)
ils seraient tombés
elles seraient tombées

PERFECT SUBJUNCTIVE

que je sois tombé(-e)
que tu sois tombé(-e)
qu'il soit tombé
qu'elle soit tombée
qu'on soit tombé
que nous soyons tombés(-es)
que vous soyez tombé(-e/-s/-es)
qu'ils soient tombés
qu'elles soient tombées

PLUPERFECT SUBJUNCTIVE

que je fusse tombé(-e)
que tu fusses tombé(-e)
qu'il fût tombé
qu'elle fût tombé
qu'on fût tombé
que nous fussions tombés(-es)
que vous fussiez tombé(-e/-s/-es)
qu'ils fussent tombés
qu'elles fussent tombées

Notes   1) The verbs which are conjugated with **être** in compound tenses are listed under the auxiliary verb itself (➤**être** *5*).

2) All compound tenses using auxiliary **être** require gender agreements on the past participle. The agreement is with the subject of the verb, and may be feminine singular (add an **-e**), masculine plural (add an **-s**), or feminine plural (add **-es**). All possible variations are given in these verb tables. The full list of possible alternatives is given here for the perfect tense; abbreviated forms are given in subsequent compound tenses.

3) A plural agreement is possible for **on est tombés**, where meaning clearly requires it.

4) **Tomber** is a regular **-er** verb.

Je *suis tombé* dans la rue.	I *fell over* in the street.
Sans la ceinture de sécurité, il *serait tombé* à l'eau.	Without the safety belt, *he would have fallen* in the water.
Elle *est tombée* amoureuse.	She'*s fallen* in love.
On m'a dit qu'il *était tombé* d'une fenêtre.	They told me he'*d fallen* out of a window.
On *est allés* à Versailles.	We *went* to Versailles.
Les enfant *sont sortis* à cinq heures.	The children *went out* at five o'clock.
Le train *est arrivé* à l'heure.	The train *arrived* on time.
Mon poisson rouge *est mort*.	My goldfish *has died*.
Vous *étiez parti* avant mon arrivée.	You *had left* before arrived.
On *était* tous *retournés* chez lui.	We *had* all *gone back* to his place.
Je *serais parti* sans lui . . .	I *would have left* without him . . .
– Où est Patrick?	– Where's Patrick?
– Il *sera parti* pour Rome.	– He'*ll have set off* for Rome.

Reflexive **-er** verb

PRESENT PARTICIPLE
me lavant /te lavant /se lavant /
nous lavant /vous lavant

PAST PARTICIPLE
lavé

IMPERATIVE
lave-toi! (tu)   lavez-vous! (vous)   lavons-nous! (nous)

PRESENT
je me lave
tu te lave
il/elle se lave
on se lave
nous nous lavons
vous vous lavez
ils/elles se lavent

PERFECT
je me suis lavé/lavée
tu t'es lavé/lavée
il s'est lavé
elle s'est lavée
on s'est lavé
nous nous sommes lavés/lavées
vous vous êtes lavé/lavée/
 lavés/lavées
ils se sont lavés
elles se sont lavées

IMPERFECT
je me lavais
tu te lavais
il/elle se lavait
on se lavait
nous nous lavions
vous vous laviez
ils/elles se lavaient

SIMPLE PAST
je me lavai
tu te lavas
il/elle se lava
on se lava
nous nous lavâmes
vous vous lavâtes
ils/elles se lavèrent

PAST PERFECT
je m'étais lavé(-e)
tu t'étais lavé(-e)
il s'était lavé
elle s'était lavée
on s'était lavé
nous nous étions lavés(-es)
vous vous étiez lavé(-e/-s/-es)
ils se sont lavés
elles se sont lavées

PAST ANTERIOR
je me fus lavé(-e)
tu te fus lavé(-e)
il se fut lavé
elle se fut lavée
on se fut lavé
nous nous fûmes lavés(-es)
vous vous fûtes lavé(-e/-s/-es)
ils se furent lavés
elles se furent lavées

FUTURE

je me laverai
tu te laveras
il/elle se lavera
on se lavera
nous nous laverons
vous vous laverez
ils/elles se laveront

CONDITIONAL

je me laverais
tu te laverais
il/elle se laverait
on se laverait
nous nous laverions
vous vous laveriez
ils/elles se laveraient

PRESENT SUBJUNCTIVE

que je me lave
que tu te laves
qu'il/elle se lave
qu'on se lave
que nous nous lavions
que vous vous laviez
qu'ils/elles se lavent

IMPERFECT SUBJUNCTIVE

que je me lavasse
que tu te lavasses
qu'il/elle se lavât
qu'on se lavât
que nous nous lavassions
que vous vous lavassiez
qu'ils/elles se lavassent

FUTURE PERFECT

je me serai lavé(-e)
tu te seras lavé(-e)
il se sera lavé
elle se sera lavée
on se sera lavé
nous nous serons lavés(-es)
vous vous serez lavé(-e/-s/-es)
ils se seront lavés
elles se seront lavées

CONDITIONAL PERFECT

je me serais lavé(-e)
tu te serais lavé(-e)
il se serait lavé
elle se serait lavée
on se serait lavé
nous nous serions lavés(-es)
vous vous seriez lavé(-e/-s/-es)
ils se seraient lavés
elles se seraient lavées

PERFECT SUBJUNCTIVE

que je me sois lavé(-e)
que te sois lavé(-e)
qu'il se soit lavé
qu'elle se soit lavée
qu'on se soit lavé
que nous nous soyons lavés(-es)
que vous vous soyez lavé(-e/-s/-es)
qu'ils se soient lavés
qu'elles se soient lavées

PLUPERFECT SUBJUNCTIVE

que je me fusse lavé (-e)
que te fusses lavé(-e)
qu'il se fût lavé
qu'elle se fût lavée
qu'on se fût lavé
que nous nous fussions lavés (-es)
que vous fussiez lavé(-e/-s/-es)
qu'ils se fussent lavés
qu'elles se fussent lavées

Notes   1) All reflexive verbs in French use **être** in compound tenses, and the rules for agreement of the past participle apply as with non-reflexive verbs using **être**, *where the reflexive pronoun is the direct object of the verb.* (In verbs where the reflexive pronoun is the indirect object, there is no agreement of the past particple.)

2) Full alternatives according to gender (masculine or feminine) and number (singular or plural) are given for the perfect tense; in the other compound tenses the alternatives are given in abbreviated form.

3) It is possible to make masculine or feminine plural agreement for **on s'est lavés/-es**, where the sense is clearly plural.

Le matin

Je *me réveille* **normalement vers sept heures. Je** *me lève* **vite. J'écoute le bulletin météo en** *me rasant.* **Puis** *je me brosse* **les dents et je** *me lave* **la figure avant de** *m'habiller.*

Elle *s'est réveillée* **vers sept heures.**

Elle *s'est demandé* **pourquoi le chien hurlait.**

Je *m'entends* **bien avec mes parents.**

Je *m'entendais* **bien avec ma grand'mère.**

Les jeunes *se sont* **bien** *amusés* **en Italie.**

Sans lui, on *se serait* **bien** *amusés.*

Installez-vous **ici, près de la fenêtre.**

Les ouvriers *s'étaient mis* **à réparer le toit.**

Recueillez-vous **un instant avant de quitter cette cathédrale.**

In the morning

I normally *wake up* around seven. I *get up* quickly. I listen to the weather report while *shaving.* Then I *brush* my teeth and *wash* my face before *getting dressed.*

She *woke up* around seven o'clock.

She *wondered* why the dog was howling.

I *get on* well with my parents.

I *used to get on* well with my grandmother.

The young people *enjoyed themselves* in Italy.

Without him, we *would have enjoyed* ourselves.

Sit here, near the window.

The workmen *had started* repairing the roof.

Meditate a moment before leaving this cathedral.

Auxiliary verb

PRESENT PARTICIPLE
ayant

PAST PARTICIPLE
eu

IMPERATIVE
aie! (tu)　　　　ayez! (vous)　　　　ayons! (nous)

PRESENT
j'ai
tu as
il/elle a
on a
nous avons
vous avez
ils/elles ont

PERFECT
j'ai eu
tu as eu
il/elle a eu
on a eu
nous avons eu
vous avez eu
ils ont eu

IMPERFECT
j'avais
tu avais
il/elle avait
on avait
nous avions
vous aviez
ils/elles avaient

SIMPLE PAST
j'eus
tu eus
il/elle eut
on eut
nous eûmes
vous eûtes
ils/elles eurent

PAST PERFECT
j'avais eu
tu avais eu
il/elle avait eu
on avait eu
nous avions eu
vous aviez eu
ils/elles avaient eu

PAST ANTERIOR
j'eus eu
tu eus eu
il/elle eut eu
on eut eu
nous eûmes eu
vous eûtes eu
ils/elles eurent eu

FUTURE
j'aurai
tu auras
il/elle aura
on aura
nous aurons
vous aurez
ils/elles auront

FUTURE PERFECT
j'aurai eu
tu auras eu
il/elle aura eu
on aura eu
nous aurons eu
vous aurez eu
ils/elles auront eu

CONDITIONAL
j'aurais
tu aurais
il/elle aurait
on aurait
nous aurions
vous auriez
ils/elles auraient

CONDITIONAL PERFECT
j'aurais eu
tu aurais eu
il/elle aurait eu
on aurait eu
nous aurions eu
vous auriez eu
ils/elles auraient eu

PRESENT SUBJUNCTIVE
que j'aie
que tu aies
qu'il/elle ait
qu'on ait
que nous ayons
que vous ayez
qu'ils/elles aient

PERFECT SUBJUNCTIVE
que j'aie eu
que tu aies eu
qu'il/elle ait eu
qu'on ait eu
que nous ayons eu
que vous ayez eu
qu'ils/elles aient eu

IMPERFECT SUBJUNCTIVE
que j'eusse
que tu eusses
qu'il/elle eût
qu'on eût
que nous eussions
que vous eussiez
qu'ils/elles eussent

PLUPERFECT SUBJUNCTIVE
que j'eusse eu
que tu eusses
qu'il/elle eût eu
qu'on eût eu
que nous eussions eu
que vous eussiez eu
qu'ils/elles eussent eu

Notes 1) **Avoir** is used as the auxiliary verb for the majority of verbs in compound tenses.
2) Note the impersonal phrase **il y a**, meaning 'there is' and 'there are' used in all common tenses. **Il y a** also means 'ago', and in this use is invariable.
Note also the idiomatic expressins using avoir: **avoir faim** (to be hungry), **avoir chaud** (to be hot), etc. ➤ Verb index.

J'*ai* dix-sept ans.	I'*m* seventeen.
Chez moi j'*ai* une machine à laver et un lave-vaisselle.	At home I *have* a washing machine and a dishwasher.

J'*ai* deux frères.	I *have* two brothers.
Quand j'étais petite, j'*avais* une belle poupée.	When I was little, I *had* a lovely doll.
En ville il y *a* deux cinémas.	In town there *are* two movie houses/cinemas.
Il y *a* deux ans je suis allé visiter le Louvre.	I went to visit the Louvre two years ago.
Il y *a eu* un accident.	There's *been* an accident.
Combien d'étudiants y *aurait*-il?	How many students *would* there *be*?
Nous *avons* besoin de votre aide.	We need your help.
J'*ai* sommeil.	I'm sleepy.
J'*ai eu* de la chance.	I've *had* some luck (I've been lucky).
Elle *aura* une soixantaine d'années.	She'll *be* about sixty.
J'*avais* peur du chien des voisins.	I *was* afraid of the neighbours' dog.
Le train partit sans qu'il *eût* le temps de lui dire au revoir.	The train left without his *having* time to say good-bye to her.

Examples of auxiliary use:

Je n'*ai* pas encore acheté de magnétoscope.	I *have*n't yet bought a video recorder.
Je n'*aurais* jamais pensé à cela.	I *would* never *have* thought of that.
Il n'*avait* pas préparé son discours.	He *had*n't prepared his speech.
Dès qu'il *eut* vu la fille, il partit.	As soon as he *had* seen the girl, he left.
Je regrette qu'il ne t'*ait* pas invité.	I'm sorry he *did*n't invite you.
Ce journaliste n'*aurait* pas écrit ça!	That journalist *would* not *have* written that!
Il *aura* fallu des années pour tout remettre en ordre.	It *will have* taken years to put everything straight.

Auxiliary verb used in some compound tenses and for the passive

IMPERATIVE
sois! (tu)   soyez! (vous)   soyons! (nous)

PRESENT
je suis
tu es
il/elle est
on est
nous sommes
vous êtes
ils/elles sont

PERFECT
j'ai été
tu as été
il/elle a été
on a été
nous avons été
vous avez été
ils/elles ont été

IMPERFECT
j'étais
tu étais
il/elle était
on était
nous étions
vous étiez
ils/elles étaient

SIMPLE PAST
je fus
tu fus
il/elle fut
on fut
nous fûmes
vous fûtes
ils/elles furent

PAST PERFECT
j'avais été
tu avais été
il/elle avait été
on avait été
nous avions été
vous aviez été
ils/elles avaient été

PAST ANTERIOR
j'eus été
tu eus été
il/elle eut été
on eut été
nous eûmes été
vous eûtes été
ils/elles eurent été

PRESENT PARTICIPLE	*PAST PARTICIPLE*
étant	été

FUTURE	*FUTURE PERFECT*
je serai	j'aurai été
tu seras	tu auras été
il/elle sera	il/elle aura été
on sera	on aura été
nous serons	nous aurons été
vous serez	vous aurez été
ils/elles seront	ils/elles auront été

CONDITIONAL	*CONDITIONAL PERFECT*
je serais	j'aurais été
tu serais	tu aurais été
il/elle serait	il/elle aurait été
on serait	on aurait été
nous serions	nous aurions été
vous seriez	vous auriez été
ils/elles seraient	ils/elles auraient été

PRESENT SUBJUNCTIVE	*PERFECT SUBJUNCTIVE*
que je sois	que j'aie été
que tu sois	que tu aies été
qu'il/elle soit	qu'il/elle ait été
qu'on soit	qu'on ait été
que nous soyons	que nous ayons été
que vous soyez	que vous ayez été
qu'ils/elles soient	qu'ils/elles aient été

IMPERFECT SUBJUNCTIVE	*PLUPERFECT SUBJUNCTIVE*
que je fusse	que j'eusse été
que tu fusses	que tu eusses été
qu'il/elle fût	qu'il/elle eût été
qu'on fût	qu'on eût été
que nous fussions	que nous eussions été
que vous fussiez	que vous eussiez été
qu'ils/elles fussent	qu'ils/elles eussent été

Notes 1) **être** is used as the auxiliary verb in compound tenses for all reflexive verbs, as well as the following 13 intransitive verbs of motion, plus their compounds:

aller	venir
partir	arriver
monter	descendre
sortir	entrer
mourir	naître
rester	retourner
tomber	

These form six pairs of verbs denoting movement in opposite directions, plus **tomber**.

2) Note that the auxiliary uses of **être** are in the formation of compound tenses, and in the passive voice (➤4c (ii), 5c (v)).

3) There is no use of this verb to create a progressive continuous present form similar to English 'I am writing'. For this, either the simple present tense is used, or the expression **être en train de faire**, if the continuity is to be stressed.

Examples of use as linking verb:

Je *suis* de nationalité britannique.	I *am* British.
Il *est* ingénieur.	He's an engineer.
Nous *sommes* très déçus.	We're very disappointed.
Les livres *sont* dans le sac.	The books *are* in the bag.
Quand j'*étais* petite, j'*étais* très timide.	When I *was* little, I *was* very shy.
Il *est* cinq heures.	It's five o'clock.
On *sera* à Paris le 20 octobre.	We'll *be* in Paris on the 20th of October.
Les chants d'oiseaux *seront* bientôt remplacés par de bruits mécaniques.	Birdsong *will* soon *be* replaced by noises of machinery.
Je *serais* très contente de partir.	I *should be* very pleased to leave.
Elle a dit qu'elle *aurait été* contente de partir.	She said she *would have been* very pleased to leave.

Auxiliary use:

Je *suis* **arrivé avant toi.**	I arrived before you.
Ils *étaient* **partis à huit heures.**	They had left at eight.
Je me *suis* **levé avant six heures.**	I got up before six.
Il ne *serait* **pas parti sans les autres.**	He wouldn't have left without the others.
Bien que je *sois* **tombé de l'échelle, je ne me** *suis* **pas fait mal.**	Although I fell off the ladder, I didn't hurt myself.
Nous *sommes* **arrivés à un point critique.**	We've reached a critical point.
Il croyait qu'on *était* **arrivés à un point critique.**	He thought we'd reached a critical point.
On se *serait* **déjà arrêtés, si le patron n'était pas arrivé!**	We would have stopped already if the boss hadn't arrived!
Ces tarifs ont *été* **négociés avec chaque chaîne.**	These rates have been negotiated with each TV channel.

Full conjugation of the passive using the verb **être**

IMPERATIVE

sois . . . (tu)   soyez . . . (vous)   soyons . . . (nous)

PRESENT
je suis blessé(-e)
tu es blessé(-e)
il est blessé
elle est blessée
on est blessé
nous sommes blessés(-es)
vous êtes blessé(-e/-s/-es)
ils sont blessés
elles sont blessées

IMPERFECT
j'étais blessé(-e)
tu étais blessé(-e)
il était blessé
elle était blessée
on était blessé
nous étions blessés(-es)
vous étiez blessé(-e/-s/-es)
ils étaient blessés
elles étaient blessées

PERFECT
j'ai été blessé(-e)
tu as été blessé(-e)
il a été blessé
elle a été blessée
on a été blessé
nous avons été blessés(-es)
vous avez été blessé(-e/-s/-es)
ils ont été blessés
elles ont été blessées

SIMPLE PAST
je fus blessé(-e)
tu fus blessé(-e)
il fut blessé
elle fut blessée
on fut blessé
nous fûmes blessés(-es)
vous fûtes blessé(-e/-s/-es)
ils furent blessés
elles furent blessées

Notes 1) The verb forms presented on other pages are all in the ordinary form, known as the 'active voice'. The 'passive voice' or 'passive' (➤5c(v)) is used when the verb's action is done to the subject by another agent, known or implied.

2) It is formed in French as in English by using the full range of tenses of the verb **être** 'to be' (➤**être** 5) and the past participle. Any transitive verb can be used passively.

3) Note again differences between the two languages where verbs do not have the same patterns of use in French as in English. A passive construction is impossible with verbs such as **donner** because, in the active version, the person receiving is not a direct object, but an indirect object.

Donner un cadeau *à* quelqu'un.   Give a present to someone.
Téléphoner *à* quelqu'un.   Telephone someone.

4) The imperative can be found occasionally.
Sois béni!   Bless you!

PRESENT PARTICIPLE
étant blessé(-e/-s/-es)

PAST PARTICIPLE
été blessé(-e/-s/-es)

PAST PERFECT
j'avais été blessé(-e)

PAST ANTERIOR
j'eus été blessé(-e)

FUTURE
je serai blessé(-e)

FUTURE PERFECT
j'aurai été blessé(-e)

CONDITIONAL
je serais blessé(-e)

CONDITIONAL PERFECT
j'aurais été blessé(-e)

PRESENT SUBJUNCTIVE
que je sois blessé(-e)

PERFECT SUBJUNCTIVE
que j'aie été blessé(-e)

IMPERFECT SUBJUNCTIVE
que je fusse blessé(-e)

PLUPERFECT SUBJUNCTIVE
que j'eusse été blessé(-e)

Je *suis aimé.*	I *am loved.*
Toutes les places *ont été prises*	All the seats *have been taken.*
Je regrette que la maison *soit vendue.*	I'm sorry the house *is sold.*
J'ai peur qu'il *ait été blessé.*	I'm afraid he'*s been injured.*
Le livre a *été retrouvé* mais il *était abîmé.*	The book *was found* but it *was ruined.*
Les fleurs *ont été données.*	The flowers *were given.*
On m'a donné les fleurs.	I was given the flowers.
On m'a téléphoné.	I was telephoned.

Regular **-er** verb

IMPERATIVE
parle! (tu)   parlez! (vous)   parlons! (nous)

PRESENT	***PERFECT***
je parle	j'ai parlé
tu parles	tu as parlé
il/elle parle	il/elle a parlé
on parle	on a parlé
nous parlons	nous avons parlé
vous parlez	vous avez parlé
ils/elles parlent	ils/elles ont parlé

IMPERFECT	***SIMPLE PAST***
je parlais	je parlai
tu parlais	tu parlas
il/elle parlait	il/elle parla
on parlait	on parla
nous parlions	nous parlâmes
vous parliez	vous parlâtes
ils/elles parlaient	ils/elles parlèrent

Similar verbs

aimer	like	**jurer**	swear
briser	break	**louer**	hire
chercher	look for	**montrer**	show
demander	ask	**oublier**	forget
écouter	listen (to)	**présenter**	present
fermer	shut	**trouver**	find
gronder	grumble	**vérifier**	check
hésiter	hesitate	**verser**	pour
inviter	invite		

Notes 1) This is the pattern for the regular **-er** verb conjugation (➤also full conjugation of **marcher** 1).
2) This is by far the largest group of verbs and is the conjugation into which newly created verbs are added.
3) On following pages are conjugations of **-er** verbs which have slight spelling modifications in certain forms.
4) **-ier** verbs follow the pattern above, which produces forms with **-ii-** in the imperfect indicative and present subjunctive:
Nous appréciions; vous appréciiez.

PRESENT PARTICIPLE	PAST PARTICIPLE
parlant	parlé

PAST PERFECT	PAST ANTERIOR
j'avais parlé	j'eus parlé

FUTURE	FUTURE PERFECT
je parlerai	j'aurai parlé

CONDITIONAL	CONDITIONAL PERFECT
je parlerais	j'aurais parlé

PRESENT SUBJUNCTIVE	PERFECT SUBJUNCTIVE
que je parle	que j'ai parlé

IMPERFECT SUBJUNCTIVE	PLUPERFECT SUBJUNCTIVE
que je parlasse	que j'eusse parlé

Conversation à sept heures du matin

– Qu'est-ce que tu *cherches*?
– Je *cherche* mon stylo. Je l'*ai laissé* sur la table.
– Alors *regarde* sous la table!
– J'y *ai* déjà *regardé*.
– Eh bien, tu *demanderas* à ta soeur! Elle te *prêtera* un stylo.
– Impossible! elle n'*acceptera* pas que j'*abîme* le stylo qu'elle *a acheté* hier matin. Pendant que j'*étudiais* ces lettres, elle *comptait* ses crayons et ses stylos!
– Si tu ne *trouves* pas ton stylo à toi, tu vas en *acheter* un autre tout de suite!

A conversation at seven o'clock in the morning

– What are you *looking for*?
– I'*m looking for* my pen. I *left* it on the table.
– Then look under the table.
– I'*ve* already *looked* there.
– Well, you *must ask* your sister. She'*ll lend* you a pen.
– Impossible. She *won't accept* me spoiling the pen she *bought* yesterday. While I *was studying* those letters, she *was counting* her pens and pencils.
– If you don't *find* your pen, you're going *to buy* another straight away.

Irregular **-er** verb

IMPERATIVE

va! (tu)   allez! (vous)   allons! (nous)

PRESENT
je vais
tu vas
il/elle va
on va
nous allons
vous allez
ils/elles vont

PERFECT
je suis allé/allée
tu es allé/allée
il est allé
elle est allée
on est allé
nous sommes allés/allées
vous êtes allé/allée/allés/allées
ils sont allés
elles sont allées

IMPERFECT
j'allais
tu allais
il/elle allait
on allait
nous allions
vous alliez
ils/elles allaient

SIMPLE PAST
j'allai
tu allas
il/elle alla
on alla
nous allâmes
vous allâtes
ils/elles allèrent

Notes   1) **Aller** is the only verb of its type, and is the only irregular **-er** verb.
2) It is used with the infinitive as an immediate future tense, like English 'I am going to do'. This form is extremely common in speech.

Examples of use as a full verb:

– Où *vas*-tu?	– Where are you going?
– Je *vais* au cinéma.	– I'm going to the movies/cinema.
– Moi, j'y *suis allée* hier.	– I went there yesterday.
– On y *serait allé* à Noël.	– We would have gone there at Christmas.

PRESENT PARTICIPLE	PAST PARTICIPLE
allant	allé

PAST PERFECT	PAST ANTERIOR
j'étais allé(-e)	je fus allé(-e)

FUTURE	FUTURE PERFECT
j'irai	je serai allé(-e)

CONDITIONAL	CONDITIONAL PERFECT
j'irais	je serais allé(-e)

PRESENT SUBJUNCTIVE	PERFECT SUBJUNCTIVE
que j'aille	que je sois allé(-e)

IMPERFECT SUBJUNCTIVE	PLUPERFECT SUBJUNCTIVE
que j'allasse	que je fusse allé(-e)

Examples of use with an infinitive to express the immediate future:

Qu'est-ce qu'on *va faire* demain?	What *are* we *going to do* tomorrow?
On *va passer* l'après-midi à la piscine.	We'*re going to spend* the afternoon at the swimming pool.
Ils *vont arriver* à midi.	They're *going to arrive* at noon/midday.
On *allait passer* l'après-midi à la plage, mais il a plu.	We were *going to spend* the afternoon at the beach, but it rained.

Regular **-er** verb doubling consonant before mute ending and in future and conditional tenses

IMPERATIVE
appelle! (tu)   appelez! (vous)   appelons! (nous)

PRESENT TENSE
j'appelle
tu appelles
il/elle appelle
on appelle
nous appelons
vous appelez
ils/elles appellent

PERFECT
j'ai appelé
tu as appelé
il/elle a appelé
on a appelé
nous avons appelé
vous avez appelé
ils ont appelé

IMPERFECT
j'appelais
tu appelais
il/elle appelait
on appelait
nous appelions
vous appeliez
ils/elles appelaient

SIMPLE PAST
j'appelai
tu appelas
il/elle appela
on appela
nous appelâmes
vous appelâtes
ils/elles appelèrent

Similar verbs

rappeler	remind	**rejeter**	reject
se rappeler	remember	**projeter**	project
jeter	throw	**ruisseler**	stream

Notes The majority of verbs in **-eler** and **-eter** are spelled this way. The doubling of the letter **-l-** or **-t-** occurs when the vowel '**e**' is an open sound, as in English 'let'; that is, when the following ending is not pronounced, and also throughout the future tense. (►**acheter** 10 for those using **è** instead of **-tt-**, **-ll-**.)

PRESENT PARTICIPLE	PAST PARTICIPLE
appelant	appelé

PAST PERFECT	PAST ANTERIOR
j'avais appelé	j'eus appelé

FUTURE	FUTURE PERFECT
j'appellerai	j'aurai appelé

CONDITIONAL	CONDITIONAL PERFECT
j'appellerais	j'aurais appelé

PRESENT SUBJUNCTIVE	PERFECT SUBJUNCTIVE
que j'appelle	que j'aie appelé

IMPERFECT SUBJUNCTIVE	PLUPERFECT SUBJUNCTIVE
que j'appelasse	que j'eusse appelé

– Je m'*appelle* Marcel.
Comment vous *appelez*-vous?

– I'm *called* Marcel.
What's your name?

Je l'ai *appelée* hier soir.

I *called* her yesterday evening.

**Je crois qu'on *rejettera*
ma suggestion.**

I think they'*ll reject* my
suggestion.

**'*Rappelle*-toi Barbara
Il pleuvait sans cesse sur
Brest ce jour-là . . .'**

'*Remember* Barbara
It was raining endlessly
on Brest that day . . .'

Paroles (Jacques Prévert)

Regular **-er** verb requiring **-è-** before mute ending and in future and conditional tenses

IMPERATIVE
achète! (tu)   achetez! (vous)   achetons! (nous)

PRESENT TENSE
j'achète
tu achètes
il/elle achète
on achète
nous achetons
vous achetez
ils/elles achètent

PERFECT
j'ai acheté
tu as acheté
il/elle a acheté
on a acheté
nous avons acheté
vous avez acheté
ils/elles ont acheté

IMPERFECT
j'achetais
tu achetais
il/elle achetait
on achetait
nous achetions
vous achetiez
ils/elles achetaient

SIMPLE PAST
j'achetai
tu achetas
il/elle acheta
on acheta
nous achetâmes
vous achetâtes
ils/elles achetèrent

Similar verbs

celer	conceal	**marteler**	hammer
ciseler	chisel	**mener**	lead
congeler	(deep-)freeze	**modeler**	model
déceler	detect	**peler**	peel
dégeler	thaw	**peser**	weigh
geler	freeze	**racheter**	buy back
haleter	pant	**semer**	sow
lever	lift	**surgeler**	deep-freeze

Notes Compounds of the verbs also follow the spelling pattern of **acheter**; **peler**; **mener**; **peser**; **lever**; and **semer**.

PRESENT PARTICIPLE achetant	**PAST PARTICIPLE** acheté
PAST PERFECT j'avais acheté	**PAST ANTERIOR** j'eus acheté
FUTURE j'achèterai	**FUTURE PERFECT** j'aurai acheté
CONDITIONAL j'achèterais	**CONDITIONAL PERFECT** j'aurais acheté
PRESENT SUBJUNCTIVE que j'achète	**PERFECT SUBJUNCTIVE** que j'aie acheté
IMPERFECT SUBJUNCTIVE que j'achetasse	**PLUPERFECT SUBJUNCTIVE** que j'eusse acheté

Je me *lève* vers sept heures. — I *get up* around seven.

Je *sème* à tout vent. — I *sow* in all directions. (Motto of Larousse publishing house.)

Tu nous *mènes* où? — Where *are* you *leading* us?

Au supermarché — *At the supermarket*

– Bonjour madame. Excusez-moi. 'J'*ai acheté* ce paquet de petits pois *congelés* hier, mais je les *ai pesés* chez moi et ils ne *pèsent* pas 200 grammes. — – Hello. Excuse me. I *bought* this packet of *frozen* peas yesterday, but I *weighed* them at home and they *don*'t *weigh* 200g.

– Désolée monsieur. Quand j'*aurai pelé* ces pommes de terre, je *me lèverai* pour vous chercher un autre paquet. — – Terribly sorry, sir. When I'*ve peeled* these potatoes, I'*ll get up* and find you another pack.

Regular -er verb changing -é- to -è-

IMPERATIVE
cède! (tu)   cédez! (vous)   cédons! (nous)

PRESENT   **PERFECT**
je cède   j'ai cédé
tu cèdes   tu as cédé
il/elle cède   il/elle a cédé
on cède   on a cédé
nous cédons   nous avons cédé
vous cédez   vous avez cédé
ils/elles cèdent   ils ont cédé

IMPERFECT   **SIMPLE PAST**
je cédais   je cédai
tu cédais   tu cédas
il/elle cédait   il/elle céda
on cédait   on céda
nous cédions   nous cédâmes
vous cédiez   vous cédâtes
ils/elles cédaient   ils/elles cédèrent

Similar verbs

accélérer	speed up	**intégrer**	include
adhérer	adhere	**interpréter**	interpret
célébrer	celebrate	**précéder**	precede
déléguer	delegate	**régler**	settle
espérer	hope	**succéder**	succeed

Notes   1) Any verb having -é- before the last syllable of the infinitive follows this pattern. There are many combinations:
-ébrer; -écer; -écher; -éder; -égler; -égner; -égrer; -éguer; -éler; -émer; -éner; -éper; -équer; -érer; -éser; -éter; -étrer; -évrer; -éyer.
2) The -è- occurs in the present tenses when the ending is not heard, and in the singular imperative.

Répétez après moi . . .	*Repeat* after me . . .
Je ne veux pas que tu **répètes** ça aux autres!	I don't want you *to repeat* that to the others!

PRESENT PARTICIPLE cédant	*PAST PARTICIPLE* cédé
PAST PERFECT j'avais cédé	*PAST ANTERIOR* j'eus cédé
FUTURE je céderai	*FUTURE PERFECT* j'aurai cédé
CONDITIONAL je céderais	*CONDITIONAL PERFECT* j'aurais cédé
PRESENT SUBJUNCTIVE que je cède	*PERFECT SUBJUNCTIVE* que j'aie cédé
IMPERFECT SUBJUNCTIVE que je cédasse	*PLUPERFECT SUBJUNCTIVE* que j'eusse cédé

Vous n'*avez* pas *complété* le travail.	You *haven't finished* the work.
J'*espérais* te voir au bureau.	I *was hoping* to see you at the office.
Il *a abrégé* son voyage.	He *cut short* his journey.
J'*interpréterai* ce vers de poésie d'après le contexte.	I *shall interpret* this line of poetry according to the context.
L'anniversaire – J'*espère* que tu *célébreras* tes vingt ans en nous invitant tous au resto!	*The birthday* – I *hope* you *will celebrate* your twentieth birthday by inviting us all to eat out!
– Bien sûr, mais je te *délègue* la responsabilité de réserver la table!	– Of course, but I'*m delegating* you to reserve the table.
– Ah bon! Et je suppose que je dois *régler* le compte après!	– Oh right! And I suppose I have to *pay* the bill after!

Regular **-er** verb ending in **-oyer** or **-uyer**

IMPERATIVE
emploie! (tu)   employez! (vous)   employons! (nous)

PRESENT
j'emploie
tu emploies
il/elle emploie
on emploie
nous employons
vous employez
ils/elles emploient

PERFECT
j'ai employé
tu as employé
il/elle a employé
on a employé
nous avons employé
vous avez employé
ils/elles ont employé

IMPERFECT
j'employais
tu employais
il/elle employait
on employait
nous employions
vous employiez
ils/elles employaient

SIMPLE PAST
j'employai
tu employas
il/elle employa
on employa
nous employâmes
vous employâtes
ils/elles employèrent

Similar verbs

appuyer	lean; press	**noyer**	drown
broyer	grind	**ployer**	bend; sag
ennuyer	bore	**tutoyer**	address Sb. as 'tu'
essuyer	wipe	**vouvoyer**	address Sb. as 'vous'

Notes   1) Verbs in **-oyer** and **-uyer** follow this pattern.
2) **Envoyer** and **renvoyer** differ in the future and conditional tenses with irregular forms: **j'enverrai/je renverrai**.

PRESENT PARTICIPLE	PAST PARTICIPLE
employant	employé

PAST PERFECT
j'avais employé

PAST ANTERIOR
j'eus employé

FUTURE
j'emploierais/j'employerais

FUTURE PERFECT
j'aurai employé

CONDITIONAL
j'emploierais/j'employerais

CONDITIONAL PERFECT
j'aurais employé

PRESENT SUBJUNCTIVE
que j'emploie/employe

PERFECT SUBJUNCTIVE
que j'aie employé

IMPERFECT SUBJUNCTIVE
que j'employasse

PLUPERFECT SUBJUNCTIVE
que j'eusse employé

J'*enverrai* ce paquet à ma soeur la semaine prochaine.
I *shall send* this package to my sister next week.

On peut se *tutoyer* maintenant.
We can *call* each other 'tu' now.

As-tu bien *essuyé* les verres?
Have you *dried* the glasses properly?

Elle m'*envoie* le journal régional tous les samedis.
She *sends* me the local paper every Saturday.

Délayez bien la farine dans le lait.
Mix the flour well into the milk.

On fait très peu pour *enrayer* le chômage.
They're not doing much *to curb* unemployment.

13 manger   eat

Regular **-er** verb ending in **-ger**

IMPERATIVE
mange! (tu)   mangez! (vous)   *mangeons*! (nous)

PRESENT
je mange
tu manges
il/elle mange
on mange
nous *mangeons*
vous mangez
ils/elles mangent

PERFECT
j'ai mangé
tu as mangé
il/elle a mangé
on a mangé
nous avons mangé
vous avez mangé
ils/elles ont mangé

IMPERFECT
je *mangeais*
tu *mangeais*
il/elle *mangeait*
on *mangeait*
nous mangions
vous mangiez
ils/elles *mangeaient*

SIMPLE PAST
je *mangeai*
tu *mangeas*
il/elle *mangea*
on *mangea*
nous *mangeâmes*
vous *mangeâtes*
ils/elles mangèrent

Similar verbs

arranger	arrange	**juger**	judge
bouger	move	**outrager**	anger
déranger	disturb	**partager**	share
enrager	enrage	**plonger**	dive
loger	house	**ranger**	dive

Notes   1) Italicized forms show the extra **-e-** in spelling.
          2) In this large group are all verbs ending in **-ger**.

PRESENT PARTICIPLE	*PAST PARTICIPLE*
mangeant	mangé

PAST PERFECT	*PAST ANTERIOR*
j'avais mangé	j'eus mangé

FUTURE	*FUTURE PERFECT*
je mangerai	j'aurai mangé

CONDITIONAL	*CONDITIONAL PERFECT*
je mangerais	j'aurais mangé

PRESENT SUBJUNCTIVE	*PERFECT SUBJUNCTIVE*
que je mange	que j'aie mangé

IMPERFECT SUBJUNCTIVE	*PLUPERFECT SUBJUNCTIVE*
que je *mangeasse*	que j'eusse mangé

Une tragédie en miniature	*A mini-tragedy*
– Qu'est-ce qu'il a, ton hamster? Il ne *bouge* plus.	– What's the matter with your hamster? He*'s* not *moving* any more.
– Je ne sais pas. Je voudrais bien qu'il *mange* quelque chose. La semaine dernière il *mangeait* très bien; mais depuis mardi il *n'a rien mangé* du tout.	– I don't know. I really wish he*'d eat* something. Last week he *was eating* very well but since Tuesday he *hasn't eaten* a thing.
– Eh bien, ramasse-le! Ça ne le *dérangera* pas.	– Well pick him up! It *won't disturb* him.
– Tu as raison. Et de toute façon il ne *rongera* plus rien. Il est mort.	– You're right. And anyway he *won't gnaw* anything else. He's dead.
Il *plongea* dans la piscine et *nagea* jusqu'à l'autre bord.	He *dived* into the swimming pool and *swam* to the other side.

14 placer **place**

Regular **-er** verb ending in **-cer**

IMPERATIVE

place! (tu)   placez! (vous)   *plaçons*! (nous)

PRESENT TENSE
je place
tu places
il/elle place
on place
nous *plaçons*
vous placez
ils/elles placent

PERFECT
j'ai placé
tu as placé
il/elle a placé
on a placé
nous avons placé
vous avez placé
ils/elles ont placé

IMPERFECT
je *plaçais*
tu *plaçais*
il/elle *plaçait*
on *plaçait*
nous placions
vous placiez
ils/elles *plaçaient*

SIMPLE PAST
je *plaçai*
tu *plaças*
il/elle *plaça*
on *plaça*
nous *plaçâmes*
vous *plaçâtes*
ils/elles placèrent

Similar verbs

annoncer	announce	**relancer**	throw back
commencer	begin	**remplacer**	replace
dénoncer	denounce	**renoncer**	renounce
effacer	rub out	**retracer**	retrace
lancer	throw; launch	**sucer**	suck
prononcer	pronounce	**tracer**	trace
recommencer	begin again		

Notes 1) The italicized forms indicate the requirement to write **ç** before vowels **a**, **o** and **u**. Hence the cedilla is written in all parts of the imperfect indicative and imperfect subjunctive; and in the simple past except in the third person plural; in the present participle; and in the first person plural present tense and imperative. (Compare the parallel use of **-ge-** in verbs of the **-ger** group ►**manger** 13 where exactly the same forms require the extra **-e-**.)
2) All verbs ending in **-cer** follow this pattern.

PRESENT PARTICIPLE plaçant	*PAST PARTICIPLE* placé
PAST PERFECT j'avais placé	*PAST ANTERIOR* j'eus placé
FUTURE je placerai	*FUTURE PERFECT* j'aurai placé
CONDITIONAL je placerais	*CONDITIONAL PERFECT* j'aurais placé
PRESENT SUBJUNCTIVE que je place	*PERFECT SUBJUNCTIVE* que j'aie placé
IMPERFECT SUBJUNCTIVE que je plaçasse	*PLUPERFECT SUBJUNCTIVE* que j'eusse placé

Commençons!

Let's begin!

C'est elle qui m'*a remplacé.*

She's the one who *replaced* me.

'Et la mer *efface* sur le sable
Les pas des amants désunis'
Les Feuilles Mortes, Jacques
Prévert

'And the sea *washes away* in the
sand the footprints of parted
lovers'

Ne *recommence* pas, je t'en
supplie!

Don't *do that again*, please.

Edward VIII *renonça* à la
couronne britannique en 1938.
Son frère le *remplaça.*

Edward VIII *renounced* the British
crown in 1938. His brother
replaced him.

Regular **-er** verb ending in **-ayer**

IMPERATIVE
pay!/paie! (tu)   payez! (vous)   payons! (nous)

PRESENT	*PERFECT*
je paye/paie	j'ai payé
tu payes/paies	tu as payé
il/elle paye/paie	il/elle a payé
on paye/paie	on a payé
nous payons	nous avons payé
vous payez	vous avez payé
ils/elles payent/paient	ils/elles ont payé

IMPERFECT	*SIMPLE PAST*
je payais	je payai
tu payais	tu payas
il/elle payait	il/elle paya
on payait	on paya
nous payions	nous payâmes
vous payiez	vous payâtes
ils/elles payaient	ils/elles payèrent

Similar verbs

déblayer	clear away	**essayer**	try
délayer	mix; thin down	**étayer**	prop up
enrayer	stop; check	**rayer**	rule; line; score out

Notes   Verbs in **-ayer** have always had the choice of spelling: either to keep the letter **-y-** throughout, or to have a letter **-i-** before silent **-e** (**-es**, **-ent**) in the present, future and conditional tenses.

PRESENT PARTICIPLE	PAST PARTICIPLE
payant	payé

PAST PERFECT	PAST ANTERIOR
j'avais payé	j'eus payé

FUTURE	FUTURE PERFECT
je payerai/paierai	j'aurai payé

CONDITIONAL	CONDITIONAL PERFECT
je payerais/paierais	j'aurais payé

PRESENT SUBJUNCTIVE	PERFECT SUBJUNCTIVE
que je paye/paie	que j'aie payé

IMPERFECT SUBJUNCTIVE	PLUPERFECT SUBJUNCTIVE
que je payasse	que j'eusse payé

Je peux *essayer* ce pantalon? — Can I *try* these pants/trousers *on*?

J'ai *payé* les billets, mais il faut que je *paie* le repas. — I've *paid* for the tickets, but I must *pay* for the meal.

Tu *essaieras de* te mettre en contact avec lui? — *Will* you *try* and contact him?

Il *a rayé* son nom. — He's *crossed* his name out.

Avant de jouer au football, nous *déblayons* le terrain. — Before playing soccer, we *are clearing* the pitch *(of obstacles)*.

Il *délaie* son discours en donnant beaucoup d'exemples. — He's *spinning out* his speech by giving lots of examples.

Regular **-ir** verb

IMPERATIVE
finis! (tu)   finissez! (vous)   finissons! (nous)

PRESENT
je finis
tu finis
il/elle finit
on finit
nous finissons
vous finissez
ils/elles finissent

IMPERFECT
je finissais
tu finissais
il/elle finissait
on finissait
nous finissions
vous finissiez
ils/elles finissaient

PAST PERFECT
j'avais fini
tu avais fini
il/elle avait fini
on avait fini
nous avions fini
vous aviez fini
ils/elles avaient fini

PERFECT
j'ai fini
tu as fini
il/elle a fini
on a fini
nous avons fini
vous avez fini
ils/elles ont fini

SIMPLE PAST
je finis
tu finis
il/elle finit
on finit
nous finîmes
vous finîtes
ils/elles finirent

PAST ANTERIOR
j'eus fini
tu eus fini
il/elle eut fini
on eut fini
nous eûmes fini
vous eûtes fini
ils/elles eurent fini

PRESENT PARTICIPLE	**PAST PARTICIPLE**
finissant	fini

PAST PERFECT   **FUTURE PERFECT**

je finirai   j'aurai fini
tu finiras   tu auras fini
il/elle finira   il/elle aura fini
on finira   on aura fini
nous finirons   nous aurons fini
vous finirez   vous aurez fini
ils/elles finiront   ils/elles auront fini

CONDITIONAL   **CONDITIONAL PERFECT**

je finirais   j'aurais fini
tu finirais   tu aurais fini
il/elle finirait   il/elle aurait
on finirait   on aurait fini
nous finirions   nous aurions fini
vous finiriez   vous auriez fini
ils/elles finiraient   ils/elles auraient fini

PRESENT SUBJUNCTIVE   **PERFECT SUBJUNCTIVE**

que je finisse   que j'aie fini
que tu finisses   que tu aies fini
qu'il/elle finisse   qu'il/elle ait fini
qu'on finisse   qu'on ait fini
que nous finissions   que nous ayons fini
que vous finissiez   que vous ayez fini
qu'ils/elles finissent   qu'ils/elles aient fini

IMPERFECT SUBJUNCTIVE **PLUPERFECT SUBJUNCTIVE**

que je finisse   que j'eusse fini
que tu finisses   que tu eusses fini
qu'il/elle finît   qu'il/elle eût fini
qu'on finît   qu'on eût fini
que nous finissions   que nous eussions fini
que vous finissiez   que vous eussiez fini
qu'ils/elles finissent   qu'ils/elles eussent fini

Similar verbs

accomplir	achieve	franchir	cross
amortir	deaden	réfléchir	reflect; ponder
applaudir	applaud	réussir	succeed
avertir	warn	surgir	appear suddenly
choisir	choose		

Change of state verbs

appauvrir	impoverish	jaunir	go yellow
blanchir	turn white	réunir	gather together
démolir	demolish	rougir	go red
enrichir	enrich	vieillir	grow old
établir	establish	unir	unite
guérir	cure; heal		

Notes   1) The regular **-ir** conjugation with **-iss-** is a large group.
2) It includes verbs implying some kind of development or change of state.

Au rayon des disques

– Les enfants, je vous *avertis* qu'on part dans deux minutes.

– Oh maman! je n'*ai* pas *fini*. Je n'*ai* rien *choisi*.

– Et moi, maman? Il faut que je *réfléchisse!* Trouver un cadeau pour Papa, ce n'est pas facile.

– Eh bien, on n'*a* pas *accompli* grand'chose ce matin.

– C'est vrai, mais si le prof ne m'*avait* pas *puni*, on aurait eu beaucoup plus de temps pour *choisir*.

On *avait établi* un petit commerce mais cela n'*a* pas *réussi*.

Les moteurs de l'avion *vrombissaient* au décollage.

Je ne voudrais pas qu'on *démolisse* le vieux musée.

At the record counter

– Children, I'*m warning* you that we're leaving in two minutes.

– Oh Mom, I *haven't finished*. I *haven't chosen* anything.

– And what about me, Mom? I have to *think about this*. Finding a present for Dad isn't easy.

– Well, we *haven't achieved* much this morning.

– That's true, but if the teacher *hadn't punished* me, we would have had a lot more time *to choose*.

They *had set up* a small business, but it *didn't succeed*.

The plane's engines *were roaring* on takeoff.

I wouldn't like them to *knock down* the old museum.

Irregular **-ir** verb

IMPERATIVE
acquiers! (tu)   acquérez! (vous)   acquérons! (nous)

PRESENT
j'acquiers
tu acquiers
il/elle acquiert
on acquiert
nous acquérons
vous acquérez
ils/elles acquièrent

PERFECT
j'ai acquis
tu as acquis
il/elle a acquis
on a acquis
nous avons acquis
vous avez acquis
ils/elles ont acquis

IMPERFECT
j'acquérais
tu acquérais
il/elle acquérait
on acquérait
nous acquérions
vous acquériez
ils/elles acquéraient

SIMPLE PAST
j'acquis
tu acquis
il/elle acquit
on acquit
nous acquîmes
vous acquîtes
ils/elles acquirent

Similar verbs

conquérir   conquer   **reconquérir**   reconquer

Notes   The main difficulties in this verb are in the present tenses, as well as
the future and conditional.

J'*ai acquis* cette table chez un brocanteur.	I *acquired* this table at a secondhand dealer's.
Où veux-tu que j'*acquière* un vélo à cette heure-ci?	Where do you expect me to *get* a bike from at this time of day?

PRESENT PARTICIPLE	*PAST PARTICIPLE*
acquérant	acquis

PAST PERFECT	*PAST ANTERIOR*
j'avais acquis	j'eus acquis

FUTURE	*FUTURE PERFECT*
j'acquerrai	j'aurai acquis

CONDITIONAL	*CONDITIONAL PERFECT*
j'acquerrais	j'aurais acquis

PRESENT SUBJUNCTIVE	*PERFECT SUBJUNCTIVE*
que j'acquière	que j'aie acquis
que tu acquières	
qu'il/elle acquière	
qu'on acquière	
que nous acquérions	
que vous acquériez	
qu'ils/elles acquièrent	

IMPERFECT SUBJUNCTIVE	*PLUPERFECT SUBJUNCTIVE*
que j'acquisse	que j'eusse acquis

Jules César *conquit* la Gaule en 58 av.J-C.	Julius Caesar *conquered* Gaul in 58 BC.
Tu *acquerras* des tableaux?	*Will* you *purchase* some paintings?
Ces antiquités *ont acquis* beaucoup de valeur.	These antiques *have appreciated* a lot in value.
Ce Lothario *conquiert* tous les coeurs des dames.	That Lothario *wins* all the ladies' hearts.
Sans la trahison, nous *aurions reconquis* notre liberté.	If we hadn't been betrayed, we *would have won back* our freedom.

Irregular **-ir** verb

IMPERATIVE
cueille! (tu)   *cueillez!* (vous)   *cueillons!* (nous)

PRESENT
je *cueille*
tu *cueilles*
il/elle cueille
on cueille
nous cueillons
vous cueillez
ils/elles cueillent

PERFECT
j'ai cueilli
tu as cueilli
il/elle a cueilli
on a cueilli
nous avons cueilli
vous avez cueilli
ils/elles ont cueilli

IMPERFECT
je *cueillais*
tu *cueillais*
il/elle *cueillait*
on *cueillait*
nous *cueillions*
vous *cueilliez*
ils/elles *cueillaient*

SIMPLE PAST
je cueillis
tu cueillis
il/elle cueillit
on cueillit
nous cueillîmes
vous cueillîtes
ils/elles cueillirent

Similar verbs

acceillir   welcome   **recueillir**   pick again

Notes 1) Italicized forms show differences from regular **-ir** verbs.
2) This group, like the **ouvrir** group, has a mixture of forms from the **-er** and **-ir** conjugations.
3) **Assaillir** 'to assail' and **défaillir** 'to faint, falter' are conjugated like **cueillir** in all forms except the future and conditional tenses, where the form is **j'assaillirai**.

'*Cueillez* dès aujourd'hui les roses de la vie'.
(Ronsard, sixteenth century)

'*Gather* today the roses of life – Gather ye rosebuds . . .'

Voici les pommes que j'*ai cueillies* ce matin.

These are the apples I *picked* this morning.

PRESENT PARTICIPLE	*PAST PARTICIPLE*
cueillant	cueilli

PAST PERFECT	*PAST ANTERIOR*
j'avais cueilli	j'eus cueilli

FUTURE
je *cueillerai*
tu *cueilleras*

FUTURE PERFECT
j'aurai cueilli

CONDITIONAL
je *cueillerais*

CONDITIONAL PERFECT
j'aurais cueilli

PRESENT SUBJUNCTIVE
que je *cueille*

PERFECT SUBJUNCTIVE
que j'aie cueilli

IMPERFECT SUBJUNCTIVE
que je cueillisse

PLUPERFECT SUBJUNCTIVE
que j'eusse cueilli

L'hôtel peut *accueillir* un grand nombre de touristes.

The hotel can *accommodate* a large number of tourists.

On m'*a accueilli* avec chaleur.

They *welcomed* me warmly.

Je l'*accueillerai* chez moi.

I *shall welcome* him into my home.

Dans six mois il *aura recueilli* son héritage.

In six months he *will have come into* his inheritance.

Le compositeur Vaughan Williams *recueillait* régulièrement les vieilles chansons folkloriques qu'il entendait.

The composer Vaughan Williams regularly *noted down* the old folk songs he heard.

On l'*a assailli* de questions après le discours.

They *bombarded* him with questions after the speech.

Elle *défaille* de faim.

She's *fainting* with hunger.

19 courir

Irregular **-ir** verb

IMPERATIVE
cours! (tu)　　　　　courez! (vous)　　　　　courons! (nous)

PRESENT
je cours
tu cours
il/elle court
on court
nous courons
vous courez
ils/elles courent

IMPERFECT
je courais
tu courais
il/elle courait
on courait
nous courions
vous couriez
ils/elles couraient

PERFECT
j'ai couru
tu as couru
il/elle a couru
on a couru
nous avons couru
vous avez couru
ils/elles ont couru

SIMPLE PAST
je courus
tu courus
il/elle courut
on courut
nous courûmes
vous courûtes
ils/elles coururent

Similar verbs

accourir	run up; rush up	**recourir**	run again
concourir	compete	**secourir**	help; assist
parcourin	cover; travel		

PRESENT PARTICIPLE	PRESENT PARTICIPLE
courant	couru

PAST PERFECT	PAST ANTERIOR
j'avais couru	j'eus couru

FUTURE	FUTURE PERFECT
je courrai	j'aurai couru

CONDITIONAL	CONDITIONAL PERFECT
je courrais	j'aurais couru

PRESENT SUBJUNCTIVE	PERFECT SUBJUNCTIVE
que je coure	que j'aie couru

IMPERFECT SUBJUNCTIVE	PLUPERFECT SUBJUNCTIVE
que je courusse	que j'eusse couru

J'*ai couru*. Je suis essoufflé.	I'*ve been running*. I'm out of breath.
Allez, *courez!*	Come on, *run!*
Il *a parcouru* le monde.	He'*s been* all over the world.
Je *recourrai* au patron.	I *shall appeal* to the boss.
On *aurait concouru* à ce projet, mais l'argent manquait.	We *would have cooperated* on that project, but money was short.
Il *secourait* toujours les amis qui avaient des problèmes financiers.	He *always helped* friends who had financial problems.

Irregular -ir verb

IMPERATIVE
dors! (tu)   dormez! (vous)   dormons (nous)

PRESENT
je *dors*
tu *dors*
il/elle *dort*
on *dort*
nous *dormons*
vous *dormez*
ils/elles *dorment*

PERFECT
j'ai dormi
tu as dormi
il/elle a dormi
on a dormi
nous avons dormi
vous avez dormi
ils/elles ont dormi

IMPERFECT
je *dormais*
tu *dormais*
il/elle *dormait*
on *dormait*
nous *dormions*
vous *dormiez*
ils/elles *dormaient*

SIMPLE PAST
je dormis
tu dormis
il/elle dormit
on dormit
nous dormîmes
vous dormîtes
ils/elles dormirent

Similar verbs

s'endormir   go to sleep   **se rendormir**   go back to sleep

Notes   Italicized forms show differences from model verb *16* - **finir**.

– *Avez*-vous bien *dormi?*

– Oui, je *me suis* très vite *endormi.* Mais mon mari ne dort jamais bien.

– Il *s'est réveillé* pendant la nuit?

– Oui, et il ne *s'est* pas *rendormi* avant six heures.

– Did you sleep well?

– Yes *I went to sleep* very quickly. But my husband never sleeps well.

– *Did* he *wake up* in the night?

– *Yes*, and he didn't *get back* to *sleep* until six o'clock.

PRESENT PARTICIPLE	*PAST PARTICIPLE*
dormant	dormi

PAST PERFECT	*PAST ANTERIOR*
j'avais dormi	j'eus dormi

FUTURE	*FUTURE PERFECT*
je dormirai	j'aurai dormi

CONDITIONAL	*CONDITIONAL PERFECT*
je dormirais	j'aurais dormit

PRESENT SUBJUNCTIVE	*PERFECT SUBJUNCTIVE*
que je *dorme*	que j'aie dormi

IMPERFECT SUBJUNCTIVE	*PLUPERFECT SUBJUNCTIVE*
que je dormisse	que j'eusse dormi

Dormez bien, les enfants!	*Sleep* well, children.
Tu dormiras bien après un petit verre de cognac.	You'*ll sleep* well after a small glass of brandy.
Ne faites pas de bruit – les gosses se seront endormis!	Don't make a noise – the kids *will have gone to sleep.*
On se serait rendormis s'il n'y avait pas eu tous ces trains qui passaient.	We *would have gone back to sleep* if there hadn't been all those trains going by.
Elle s'était vite endormie.	She *had fallen asleep* quickly.

Irregular **-ir** verb

IMPERATIVE
—

PRESENT	*PERFECT*
—	j'ai failli
	tu as failli
	il/elle a failli
	on a failli
	nous avons failli
	vous avez failli
	ils/elles ont failli

IMPERFECT	*SIMPLE PAST*
—	je faillis
	tu faillis
	il/elle faillit
	on faillit
	nous faillîmes
	vous faillîtes
	ils/elles faillirent

Notes   This verb exists only in past tenses.

PRESENT PARTICIPLE	*PAST PARTICIPLE*
faillant	failli

PAST PERFECT	*PAST ANTERIOR*
j'avais failli	j'eus failli

FUTURE	*FUTURE PERFECT*
—	j'aurai failli

CONDITIONAL	*CONDITIONAL PERFECT*
—	j'aurais failli

PRESENT SUBJUNCTIVE	*PERFECT SUBJUNCTIVE*
—	que j'aie failli

IMPERFECT SUBJUNCTIVE	*PLUPERFECT SUBJUNCTIVE*
—	que j'eusse failli

J'*ai failli* réussir.	I *almost* succeeded.
Il *a failli* tomber.	He *almost* fell.
On *a failli* perdre tout notre argent.	We *nearly* lost all our money.

Note: *faillir à quelque chose* – to be lacking; fail in

Il *faillit* à son devoir.	He *failed* in his duty.
Son courage lui *faillit*.	Her courage *failed* her.

Irregular **-ir** verb

IMPERATIVE
fuis! (tu)   fuyez! (vous)   fuyons! (nous)

### PRESENT	### PERFECT
je fuis	j'ai fui
tu fuis	tu as fui
il/elle fuit	il/elle a fui
on fuit	on a fui
nous fuyons	nous avons fui
vous fuyez	vous avez fui
ils/elles fuient	ils/elles ont fui

### IMPERFECT	### SIMPLE PAST
je fuyais	je fuis
tu fuyais	tu fuis
il/elle fuyait	il/elle fuit
on fuyait	on fuit
nous fuyions	nous fuîmes
vous fuyiez	vous fuîtes
ils/elles fuyaient	ils/elles fuirent

Similar verbs

s'enfuir   run away; flee

Notes   1) The **-y-** in forms with an audible ending is the main feature of this verb.
2) **S'enfuir** 'flee from; run away' is conjugated in the same way (with **être** in compound tenses).

PRESENT PARTICIPLE fuyant	*PAST PARTICIPLE* fui

PAST PERFECT j'avais fui	*PAST ANTERIOR* j'eus fui
FUTURE je fuirai	*FUTURE PERFECT* j'aurai fui
CONDITIONAL je fuirais	*CONDITIONAL PERFECT* j'aurais fui
PRESENT SUBJUNCTIVE que je fuie	*PERFECT SUBJUNCTIVE* que j'aie fui
IMPERFECT SUBJUNCTIVE que je fuisse	*PLUPERFECT SUBJUNCTIVE* que j'eusse fui

Fuyons!	Let's *run for it!*
Il *s'est enfui* à toute vitesse.	He *ran away* as fast as he could.
Les réfugiés *fuient* devant les soldats.	The refugees *are fleeing* from the soldiers.
Le temps *fuit.*	Time *flies.*
Le beau temps *a fui.*	The fine weather's *gone.*

Irregular -ir verb

IMPERATIVE
meurs! (tu)   mourez! (vous)   mourons! (nous)

PRESENT
je meurs
tu meurs
il/elle meurt
on meurt
nous mourons
vous mourez
ils/elles meurent

PERFECT
je suis mort
tu es mort
il est mort/elle est morte
on est mort
nous sommes morts
vous êtes mort(-e/-s/-es)
ils sont morts/elles sont mortes

IMPERFECT
je mourais
tu mourais
il/elle mourait
on mourait
nous mourions
vous mouriez
ils/elles mouraient

SIMPLE PAST
je mourus
tu mourus
il/elle mourut
on mourut
nous mourûmes
vous mourûtes
ils/elles moururent

Notes   1) The present tenses and the future and conditional are irregular
forms, as well as the simple past and imperfect subjunctive.
2) The past participle is irregular but well known in its use as the
adjective 'dead'.
3) **Mourir** takes **être** in compound tenses, as does **naître** 'to be born'.

Il *est mort*.	He is *dead/has died*.
Jeanne d'Arc *mourut* en **1431**.	Joan of Arc *died* in 1431.
On *a failli mourir* de **peur**.	We *nearly died* of fright.
C'est *à mourir* de rire.	It's *enough to make you die* laughing.
Il *devait mourir* **plus tard** de ses blessures.	He *was to die* later from his wounds.
On attend qu'il *meure*.	We're waiting for him to *die*.

PRESENT PARTICIPLE mourant	*PAST PARTICIPLE* mort

PAST PERFECT j'étais mort(-e)	*PAST ANTERIOR* je fus mort(-e)
FUTURE je mourrai	*FUTURE PERFECT* je serai mort(-e)
CONDITIONAL je mourrais	*CONDITIONAL PERFECT* je serais mort(-e)
PRESENT SUBJUNCTIVE que je meure	*PERFECT SUBJUNCTIVE* que je sois mort(-e)
IMPERFECT SUBJUNCTIVE que je mourusse	*PLUPERFECT SUBJUNCTIVE* que je fusse mort(-e)

Sans les soins de mon médicin, je *serais mort* il y a bien longtemps.	Without my doctor's care, I *would have died* ages ago.
Bien des enfants du Tiers Monde *meurent* avant l'âge de cinq ans.	Many children in the Third World *die* before the age of five.
Quelle tragédie que Chopin *soit mort* si jeune!	What a tragedy that Chopin *died* so young!

Irregular **-ir** verb

IMPERATIVE
ouvre! (tu)   *ouvrez!* (vous)   *ouvrons!* (nous)

PRESENT
j'*ouvre*
tu *ouvres*
il/elle *ouvre*
on *ouvre*
nous *ouvrons*
vous *ouvrez*
ils/elles *ouvrent*

PERFECT
j'ai *ouvert*
tu as *ouvert*
il/elle a *ouvert*
on a *ouvert*
nous avons *ouvert*
vous avez *ouvert*
ils/elles ont *ouvert*

IMPERFECT
j'*ouvrais*
tu *ouvrais*
il/elle *ouvrait*
on *ouvrait*
nous *ouvrions*
vous *ouvriez*
ils/elles *ouvraient*

SIMPLE PAST
j'ouvris
tu ouvris
il/elle ouvrit
on ouvrit
nous ouvrîmes
vous ouvrîtes
ils/elles ouvrirent

Similar verbs

couvrir	cover	**rouvrir**	open again
découvrir	discover	**souffrir**	suffer
offrir	offer		

Notes   1) Italicized forms show differences from model verb *16* – **finir**.
2) This group displays a mixture of forms from the **-er** and **-ir** conjugations.

PRESENT PARTICIPLE
ouvrant

PAST PARTICIPLE
ouvert

PAST PERFECT
j'avais *ouvert*

PAST ANTERIOR
j'eus *ouvert*

FUTURE
j'ouvrirai

FUTURE PERFECT
j'aurai *ouvert*

CONDITIONAL
j'ouvrirais

CONDITIONAL PERFECT
j'aurais *ouvert*

PRESENT SUBJUNCTIVE
que j'*ouvre*
que tu *ouvres*

PERFECT SUBJUNCTIVE
que j'aie *ouvert*

IMPERFECT SUBJUNCTIVE
que j'ouvrisse

PLUPERFECT SUBJUNCTIVE
que j'eusse *ouvert*

Ouvrez les fenêtres!

Open the windows!

Qu'est-ce qu'on t'*a offert* comme cadeau?

What present *did* they *give* you?

D'ici on *découvre* toute la ville.

You *can see* the whole town from here.

La police *a découvert* deux kilos de cannabis dans la voiture.

The police *discovered* two kilos of cannabis in the car.

Va *ouvrir!*

Go and *open* the door!

Le bureau *ouvre* à quelle heure?

What time *does* the office *open?*

Il nous *offrait* de séjourner chez lui.

He *was offering* us a stay at his house.

Maintenant il *aura découvert* son erreur.

He *will have discovered* his mistake by now.

Irregular **-ir** verb

IMPERATIVE

sens! (tu) *sentez!* (vous) *sentons!* (nous)

PRESENT
je *sens*
tu *sens*
il/elle *sent*
on *sent*
nous *sentons*
vous *sentez*
ils/elles *sentent*

PERFECT
j'ai senti
tu as senti
il/elle a senti
on a senti
nous avons senti
vous avez senti
ils/elles ont senti

IMPERFECT
je *sentais*
tu *sentais*
il/elle *sentait*
on *sentait*
nous *sentions*
vous *sentiez*
ils/elles *sentaient*

SIMPLE PAST
je sentis
tu sentis
il/elle sentit
on sentit
nous sentîmes
vous sentîtes
ils/elles sentirent

Similar verbs

mentir	lie; tell lies	**se repentir**	repent
partir	leave; go away	**sortir**	go out
ressentir	feel; experience		

Notes 1) Italicized forms show differences from model verb *16* – **finir**.
2) **Sortir** and **partir**, plus their compounds, are also in this group,
though these are all conjugated with **être** in compound tenses.

PRESENT PARTICIPLE	PAST PARTICIPLE
sentant	senti

PAST PERFECT	PAST ANTERIOR
j'avais senti	j'eus senti

FUTURE	FUTURE PERFECT
je sentirai	j'aurai senti

CONDITIONAL	CONDITIONAL PERFECT
je sentirais	j'aurais senti

PRESENT SUBJUNCTIVE	PERFECT SUBJUNCTIVE
que je *sente*	que j'aie senti
que tu *sentes*	
qu'il/elle *sente*	

IMPERFECT SUBJUNCTIVE	PLUPERFECT SUBJUNCTIVE
que je *sentisse*	que j'eusse senti

Je ne *me sens* pas très bien aujourd'hui.	I don't *feel* very well today.
Ce n'est pas vrai – tu m'*as menti.*	It isn't true – you *lied* to me.
. . . il est permis de *mentir* aux enfants quand c'est pour leur bien. *La Gloire de Mon Père (Marcel Pagnol)*	. . . you are allowed *to lie* to children when it's for their own good.
'*Repens-toi*, Dieu te pardonnera!' *(Line from traditional song about St Nicholas)*	'*Repent*, God will forgive you!'
Il *est sorti* tout à l'heure.	He *went out* just now.
Le bateau *partira* à quatorze heures.	The boat *will leave* at 2.00 p.m.

Irregular **-ir** verb

IMPERATIVE
tiens! (tu)   tenez! (vous)   tenons! (nous)

PRESENT
je tiens
tu tiens
il/elle tient
on tient
nous tenons
vous tenez
ils/elles tiennent

PERFECT
j'ai tenu
tu as tenu
il/elle a tenu
on a tenu
nous avons tenu
vous avez tenu
ils/elles ont tenu

IMPERFECT
je tenais
tu tenais
il/elle tenait
on tenait
nous tenions
vous teniez
ils/elles tenaient

SIMPLE PAST
je tins
tu tins
il/elle tint
on tint
nous tînmes
vous tîntes
ils/elles tinrent

PAST PERFECT
j'avais tenu

PAST ANTERIOR
j'eus tenu

Similar verbs

abstenir (s')	refrain; abstain	**maintenir**	maintain
appartenir	belong	**obtenir**	obtain
contenir	contain; hold; take	**retenir**	hold back
détenir	detain; hold	**soutenir**	support;
entretenir	maintain; keep; support		sustain

Notes   1) **Venir** and all its compounds are also in this group, but are conjugated with **être** in compound tenses (except **prévenir**, which is conjugated with **avoir**). Compounds are **convenir**; **devenir**; **intervenir**; **souvenir (se)**; **survenir**; and **redevenir**.
2) **Venir de faire** is an idiomatic expression meaning 'to have done'.

PRESENT PARTICIPLE	*PAST PARTICIPLE*
tenant	tenu

FUTURE	*FUTURE PERFECT*
je tiendrai	j'aurai tenu

CONDITIONAL	*CONDITIONAL PERFECT*
je tiendrais	j'aurais tenu

PRESENT SUBJUNCTIVE
que je tienne
que tu tiennes
qu'il/elle tienne
qu'on tienne
que nous tenions
que vous teniez
qu'ils/elles tiennent

PERFECT SUBJUNCTIVE
que j'aie tenu

IMPERFECT SUBJUNCTIVE
que je tinsse
que tu tinsses
qu'il tînt
que nous tinssions
que vous tinssiez
qu'ils/elles tinssent

PLUPERFECT SUBJUNCTIVE
que j'eusse tenu

Tu *viens* avec moi?

Are you *coming* with me?

Il *tenait à* faire votre connaissance.

He really *wanted to* meet you.

Il *est devenu* facteur.

He *became* a mailman/postman.

Demain il va *soutenir* sa thèse.

Tomorrow he's *going for* his viva.

Je ne sais pas ce qui *me retient* de vous casser la figure.
La Gloire de mon père (Marcel Pagnol)

I don't know what'*s stopping* me from smashing your face in.

Examples of the use of **venir de faire:**
Le train *venait de partir*.

The train *had just left.*

'*Vient de paraître*'.

Just out/just published.

Irregular **-ir** verb

IMPERATIVE
vêts! (tu)   vêtez! (vous)   vêtons! (nous)

PRESENT
je vêts
tu vêts
il/elle vêt
on vêt
nous vêtons
vous vêtez
ils/elles vêtent

PERFECT
j'ai vêtu
tu as vêtu
il/elle a vêtu
on a vêtu
nous avons vêtu
vous avez vêtu
ils/elles ont vêtu

IMPERFECT
je vêtais
tu vêtais
il/elle vêtait
on vêtait
nous vêtions
vous vêtiez
ils/elles vêtaient

SIMPLE PAST
je vêtis
tu vêtis
il/elle vêtit
on vêtit
nous vêtîmes
vous vêtîtes
ils/elles vêtirent

Similar verbs

dévêtir   undress   **revêtir**   put on; take on

Notes The reflexive verb means 'to get dressed', and is more usual with compound tenses conjugated with **être**, in common with all reflexive verbs.

PRESENT PARTICIPLE vêtant	**PAST PARTICIPLE** vêtu

PAST PERFECT j'avais vêtu	**PAST ANTERIOR** j'eus vêtu
FUTURE je vêtirai	**FUTURE PERFECT** j'aurai vêtu
CONDITIONAL je vêtirais	**CONDITIONAL PERFECT** j'aurais vêtu
PRESENT SUBJUNCTIVE que je vête	**PERFECT SUBJUNCTIVE** que j'aie vêtu
IMPERFECT SUBJUNCTIVE que je vêtisse	**PLUPERFECT SUBJUNCTIVE** que j'eusse vêtu

Elle *s'est vêtue* en noir.	She *dressed* in black.
Revêts-toi vite!	*Get dressed again* quickly!

Regular **-re** verb

IMPERATIVE

vends! (tu)　　　　vendez! (vous)　　　　vendons! (nous)

PRESENT

je vends
tu vends
il/elle vend
on vend
nous vendons
vous vendez
ils/elles vendent

PERFECT

j'ai vendu
tu as vendu
il/elle a vendu
on a vendu
nous avons vendu
vous avez vendu
ils/elles ont vendu

IMPERFECT

je vendais
tu vendais
il/elle vendait
on vendait
nous vendions
vous vendiez
ils/elles vendaient

SIMPLE PAST

je vendis
tu vendis
il/elle vendit
on vendit
nous vendîmes
vous vendîtes
ils/elles vendirent

PAST PERFECT

j'avais vendu
tu avais vendu
il/elle avait vendu
on avait vendu
nous avions vendu
vous aviez vendu
ils/elles avaient vendu

PAST ANTERIOR

j'eus vendu
tu eus vendu
il/elle eut vendu
on eut vendu
nous eûmes vendu
vous eûtes vendu
ils/elles eurent vendu

PRESENT PARTICIPLE
vendant

PAST PARTICIPLE
vendu

FUTURE
je vendrai
tu vendras
il/elle vendra
on vendra
nous vendrons
vous vendrez
ils/elles vendront

FUTURE PERFECT
j'aurai vendu
tu auras vendu
il/elle aura vendu
on aura vendu
nous aurons vendu
vous aurez vendu
ils/elles auront vendu

CONDITIONAL
je vendrais
tu vendrais
il/elle vendrait
on vendrait
nous vendrions
vous vendriez
ils/elles vendraient

CONDITIONAL PERFECT
j'aurais vendu
tu aurais vendu
il/elle aurait vendu
on aurait vendu
nous aurions vendu
vous auriez vendu
ils/elles auraient vendu

PRESENT SUBJUNCTIVE
que je vende
que tu vendes
qu'il/elle vende
qu'on vende
que nous vendions
que vous vendiez
qu'ils/elles vendent

PERFECT SUBJUNCTIVE
que j'aie vendu
que tu aies vendu
qu'il/elle ait vendu
qu'on ait vendu
que nous ayons vendu
que vous ayez vendu
qu'ils/elles aient vendu

IMPERFECT SUBJUNCTIVE
que je vendisse
que tu vendisses
qu'il/elle vendît
qu'on vendît
que nous vendissions
que vous vendissiez
qu'ils/elles vendissent

PLUPERFECT SUBJUNCTIVE
que j'eusse vendu
que tu eusses vendu
qu'il/elle eût vendu
qu'on eût vendu
que nous eussions vendu
que vous eussiez vendu
qu'ils/elles eussent vendu

Similar verbs

attendre	wait (for)	**prétendre**	claim
dépendre	depend	**répandre**	spread
descendre	go down (►Index, page 174)	**répondre**	answer
		rendre	give back; render
entendre	hear	**suspendre**	hang; suspend
pendre	hang	**tondre**	cut (lawn)
pondre	lay (eggs)		

Notes 1) A large group of verbs follows this pattern of the regular **-re** conjugation.

2) There are, however, a lot of verbs with infinitives in **-re** which are irregular.

3) **Rompre** 'to break' is conjugated like **vendre**, except that the third person singular of the present tense is **il rompt**, **etc**. Compounds **corrompre** and **interrompre** follow this pattern.

4) **Vaincre** 'to win, conquer' is conjugated like **vendre**, except that it requires **-qu-** in the plural of the present indicative; and in all parts of the imperfect tenses, the simple past and the present subjunctive. **Convaincre** (to convince) has the same forms.

– Qu'est-ce que vous *attendez?*	– What are you *waiting for?*
– J'*ai entendu dire* qu'on va vendre des cassettes et des CD ici au marché.	– I've heard they're going to sell cassettes and CDs here in the market.
– C'*est* vrai? A quelle heure?	– *Is* that right? What time?
– Je ne sais pas. Ça *dépend* . . .	– I don't know. It *depends* . . .

29 boire drink

Irregular **-re** verb

IMPERATIVE

bois! (tu)   buvez! (vous)   buvons! (nous)

PRESENT

je bois

tu bois

il/elle boit

on boit

nous buvons

vous buvez

ils/elles boivent

IMPERFECT

je buvais

tu buvais

il/elle buvait

on buvait

nous buvions

vous buviez

ils/elles buvaient

PERFECT

j'ai bu

tu as bu

il/elle a bu

on a bu

nous avons bu

vous avez bu

ils/elles ont bu

SIMPLE PAST

je bus

tu bus

il/elle but

on but

nous bûmes

vous bûtes

ils/elles burent

Notes This is the only verb of its type.

PRESENT PARTICIPLE	PAST PARTICIPLE
buvant	bu

PAST PERFECT	PAST ANTERIOR
j'avais bu	j'eus bu

FUTURE	FUTURE PERFECT
je boirai	j'aurai bu

CONDITIONAL	CONDITIONAL PERFECT
je boirais	j'aurais

PRESENT SUBJUNCTIVE	PERFECT SUBJUNCTIVE
que je boive	que j'aie bu

IMPERFECT SUBJUNCTIVE	PLUPERFECT SUBJUNCTIVE
que je busse	que j'eusse bu

J'en *boirai* cinq ou six bouteilles (Traditional song *Chevaliers de la table ronde*)	. . I'*ll drink* five or six bottles . . .
Il *a* trop *bu.*	He'*s had* too much to *drink.*
Tu *bois* du thé?	*Do* you *drink* tea?
Je ne *bois* pas d'alcool.	I *don't drink* (alcoholic drinks).
Tant il *but* et mangea, le pauvre saint homme, qu'il mourut pendant la nuit . . . *Lettres de mon moulin* ('Les Trois Messes basses') (Alphonse Daudet)	So much *did* he eat and *drink,* the poor holy man, that he died during the night . . .

Irregular **-re** verb

IMPERATIVE
conclus! (tu)   concluez! (vous)   concluons! (nous)

PRESENT
je conclus
tu conclus
il/elle conclut
on conclut
nous concluons
vous concluez
ils/elles concluent

PERFECT
j'ai conclu
tu as conclu
il/elle a conclu
on a conclu
nous avons conclu
vous avez conclu
ils/elles ont conclu

IMPERFECT
je concluais
tu concluais
il/elle concluait
on concluait
nous concluions
vous concluiez
ils/elles concluaient

SIMPLE PAST
je conclus
tu conclus
il/elle conclut
on conclut
nous conclûmes
vous conclûtes
ils/elles conclurent

Similar verbs

exclure   turn; put out   **inclure**   insert; include

Notes **Inclure** 'insert; include' is conjugated like **conclure**, the only differences being that the past participle is **inclus**.

PRESENT PARTICIPLE	*PAST PARTICIPLE*
concluant	conclu

PAST PERFECT	*PAST ANTERIOR*
j'avais conclu	j'eus conclu

FUTURE	*FUTURE PERFECT*
je conclurai	j'aurai conclu

CONDITIONAL	*CONDITIONAL PERFECT*
je conclurais	j'aurais conclu

PRESENT SUBJUNCTIVE	*PERFECT SUBJUNCTIVE*
que je conclue	que j'aie conclu

IMPERFECT SUBJUNCTIVE	*PLUPERFECT SUBJUNCTIVE*
que je conclusse	que j'eusse conclu

Marché *conclu!*	It's a deal!
Les jurés *ont conclu* à sa culpabilité.	The jury *decided* he was guilty.
Vous trouverez *ci-inclus* ledossier que j'ai préparé.	You will find *enclosed* the file I prepared.
On *conclut* le traité de Versailles en 1919.	The treaty of Versailles *was signed* in 1919.
J'*ai conclu* mon article endonnant des statistiques.	I'*ve concluded* my article by giving some statistics.
On *exclut* votre participation à ce projet.	They *are refusing* to let you join in this project.
Il n'*est* pas *exclu* que je fasse partie du groupe.	It'*s* not *out of the question* for me to join the group.

Irregular **-re** verb ending in **-uire**

IMPERATIVE
conduis! (tu)   conduisez! (vous)   conduisons! (nous)

PRESENT
je conduis
tu conduis
il/elle conduit
on conduit
nous conduisons
vous conduisez
ils/elles conduisent

PERFECT
j'ai conduit
tu as conduit
il/elle a conduit
on a conduit
nous avons conduit
vous avez conduit
ils/elles ont conduit

IMPERFECT
je conduisais
tu conduisais
il/elle conduisait
on conduisait
nous conduisions
vous conduisiez
ils/elles conduisaient

SIMPLE PAST
je conduisis
tu conduisis
il/elle conduisit
on conduisit
nous conduisîmes
vous conduisîtes
ils/elles conduisirent

Similar verbs

construire	construct; build	**nuire**	harm
cuire	cook	**produire**	produce
introduire	introduce	**réduire**	reduce
luire	gleam; shine	**traduire**	translate

Notes   1) Verbs in this group include compounds of the verbs listed here (e.g. **reconstruire**).
2) The past participles of **luire** and **nuire** are **lui** and **nui**.

Au restaurant

– **Et le steak, vous le** *prenez* **comment?**
– **Bien** *cuit.*

At the restaurant

– How would you *like* your steak?

– Well *done*.

PRESENT PARTICIPLE	*PAST PARTICIPLE*
conduisant	conduit

PAST PERFECT	*PAST ANTERIOR*
j'avais conduit	j'eus conduit

FUTURE	*FUTURE PERFECT*
je conduirai	j'aurai conduit

CONDITIONAL	*CONDITIONAL PERFECT*
je conduirais	j'aurais conduit

PRESENT SUBJUNCTIVE	*PERFECT SUBJUNCTIVE*
que je conduise	que j'aie conduit

IMPERFECT SUBJUNCTIVE	*PLUPERFECT SUBJUNCTIVE*
que je conduisisse	que j'eusse conduit

Sur la grand route	*On the road*
– Tiens! Je ne savais pas qu'on *avait construit* cet immeuble!	– Well, I'll be! I didn't know they'*d built* that apartment house.
– Oui, c'est une compagnie italienne qui l'*a construit* et c'est moi qui *ai traduit* touts les documents.	– Yes it's an Italian company that *built it*, and I was the one who *translated* all the documents.
– Ah bon? Mais tu *conduis* trop vite, tu sais.	– Oh yes? But you'*re driving* too fast, you know.
– Quelle est cette lumière qui *luit* là-bas?	– What's that light *glowing* over there?
– Je crois que c'est un *ver luisant*.	– I think it's a *glow-worm*.

Irregular **-re** verb

IMPERATIVE

connais! (tu)   connaissez! (vous)   connaissons! (nous)

PRESENT

je connais
tu connais
il/elle connaît
on connaît
nous connaissons
vous connaissez
ils connaissent

PERFECT

j'ai connu
tu as connu
il/elle a connu
on a connu
nous avons connu
vous avez connu
ils/elles ont connu

IMPERFECT

je connaissais
tu connaissais
il/elle connaissait
on connaissait
nous connaissions
vous connaissiez
ils/elles connaissaient

SIMPLE PAST

je connus
tu connus
il/elle connut
on connut
nous connûmes
vous connûtes
ils/elles connurent

Similar verbs

apparaître   appear
comparaître   compare
disparaître   disappear
reconnaître   recognise

Notes   All compounds of **connaître** and **paraître** follow the pattern of **connaître**.

PRESENT PARTICIPLE	PAST PARTICIPLE
connaissant	connu

PAST PERFECT	PAST ANTERIOR
j'avais connu	j'eus connu

FUTURE	FUTURE PERFECT
je connaîtrai	j'aurai connu

CONDITIONAL	CONDITIONAL PERFECT
je connaîtrais	j'aurais connu

PRESENT SUBJUNCTIVE	PERFECT SUBJUNCTIVE
que je connaisse	que j'aie connu

IMPERFECT SUBJUNCTIVE	PLUPERFECT SUBJUNCTIVE
que je connusse	que j'eusse connu

Les causes de ce désastre ne *sont* pas encore *connues*.	The causes of this disaster aren't yet *known*.
Tu *connais* cet homme?	*Do* you *know* that man?
Il l'*a connue* à Paris.	He *met her* in Paris.
Je la *connaissais* déjà depuis cinq ans.	I'*d* already *known* her for five years.
Il doit *comparaître* devant le tribunal.	He has *to appear* before the court.
Je n'ai jamais su comment ils *s'étaient connus* . . . *La Gloire de mon père (Marcel Pagnol)*	I never found out how they *had got to know each other* . . .

Irregular **-re** verb

IMPERATIVE
couds! (tu)   cousez! (vous)   cousons! (nous)

PRESENT
je couds
tu couds
il/elle coud
on coud
nous cousons
vous cousez
ils/elles cousent

PERFECT
j'ai cousu
tu as cousu
il/elle a cousu
on a cousu
nous avons cousu
nous avez cousu
ils/elles ont cousu

IMPERFECT
je cousais
tu cousais
il/elle cousait
on cousait
nous cousions
vous cousiez
ils/elles cousaient

SIMPLE PAST
je cousis
tu cousis
il/elle cousit
on cousit
nous cousîmes
vous cousîtes
ils/elles cousirent

Similar verbs

découdre   unpick
recoudre   sew up/back on again

PRESENT PARTICIPLE	*PAST PARTICIPLE*
cousant	cousu

PAST PERFECT	*PAST ANTERIOR*
j'avais cousu	j'eus cousu

FUTURE
je coudrai

FUTURE PERFECT
j'aurai cousu

CONDITIONAL
je coudrais

CONDITIONAL PERFECT
j'aurais cousu

PRESENT SUBJUNCTIVE
que je couse

PERFECT SUBJUNCTIVE
que j'aie cousu

IMPERFECT SUBJUNCTIVE
que je cousisse

PLUPERFECT SUBJUNCTIVE
que j'eusse cousu

Elle *a cousu* le bouton à la chemise.

She *sewed* the button on the shirt.

Tu pourrais me *recoudre* cet ourlet?

Could you *sew up* this seam *again* for me?

Elle *coud* une robe.

She's *making* a dress.

Elle *avait recousu* tout le devant de la jupe.

She *had re-sewn* all the front of the skirt.

Je *découdrais* tout ça, si j'avais le temps.

I'd *undo* all that stitching, if I had the time.

Irregular **-re** verb

IMPERATIVE
crois! (tu)   croyez! (vous)   croyons! (nous)

PRESENT
je crois
tu crois
il/elle croit
on croit
nous croyons
vous croyez
ils/elles croient

PERFECT
j'ai cru
tu as cru
il/elle a cru
on a cru
nous avons cru
vous avez cru
ils/elles ont cru

IMPERFECT
je croyais
tu croyais
il/elle croyait
on croyait
nous croyions
vous croyiez
ils/elles croyaient

SIMPLE PAST
je crus
tu crus
il/elle crut
on crut
nous crûmes
vous crûtes
ils/elles crurent

Notes   This is the only verb of this type.

PRESENT PARTICIPLE	*PAST PARTICIPLE*
croyant	cru

PAST PERFECT	*PAST ANTERIOR*
j'avais cru	j'eus cru
FUTURE	*FUTURE PERFECT*
je croirai	j'aurai cru
CONDITIONAL	*CONDITIONAL PERFECT*
je croirais	j'aurais cru
PRESENT SUBJUNCTIVE	*PERFECT SUBJUNCTIVE*
que je croie	que j'aie cru
que nous croyions	
IMPERFECT SUBJUNCTIVE	*PLUPERFECT SUBJUNCTIVE*
que je crusse	que j'eusse cru

– Tu *crois* qu'il arrivera bientôt?	– *Do* you *think* he'll arrive soon?
– Non, je ne *crois* pas.	– No, I *don't think* so.
Je *croyais* qu'il allait te prêter 1.000 francs.	I thought he was going to lend you 1,000 francs.
Croyez-vous en Dieu?	*Do* you *believe* in God?
Je n'*aurais* pas *cru* . . .	I *wouldn't have thought* . . .

Irregular **-re** verb

IMPERATIVE

dis! (tu)   dites! (vous)   disons! (nous)

PRESENT
je dis
tu dis
il/elle dit
on dit
nous disons
vous dites
ils/elles disent

PERFECT
j'ai dit
tu as dit
il/elle a dit
on a dit
nous avons dit
vous avez dit
ils/elles ont dit

IMPERFECT
je disais
tu disais
il/elle disait
on disait
nous disions
vous disiez
ils/elles disaient

SIMPLE PAST
je dis
tu dis
il/elle dit
on dit
nous dîmes
vous dîtes
ils/elles dirent

Similar verbs

contredire	contradict
interdire	forbid; prohibit
frire	fry
prédire	foretell; predict

Notes   1) Similarities with and differences from **écrire** and **lire** will be obvious.
2) **Suffire** (be sufficient) is conjugated like **dire**, except that the present indicative tense has **vous suffisez**, and the past participle is **suffi**.
3) **Frire** 'fry' is another similar verb, which is found mainly in the past participle, **frit** 'fried', and the expression **faire frire** 'fry food'.

Que *dis*-tu?	What *do* you *say?* What *are* you *saying?*
Je lui *ai dit* de venir me voir.	I *told* him to come and see me.
***Dites*-lui bonjour de ma part.**	*Say* hello to her from me.

PRESENT PARTICIPLE	*PAST PARTICIPLE*
disant	dit

PAST PERFECT	*PAST ANTERIOR*
j'avais dit	j'eus dit

FUTURE	*FUTURE PERFECT*
je dirai	j'aurai dit

CONDITIONAL	*CONDITIONAL PERFECT*
je dirais	j'aurais dit

PRESENT SUBJUNCTIVE	*PERFECT SUBJUNCTIVE*
que je dise	que j'aie dit

IMPERFECT SUBJUNCTIVE	*PLUPERFECT SUBJUNCTIVE*
que je disse	que j'eusse dit

Il n'*a* rien *dit*.	He di*d*n't *say* a thing. (He *said* nothing.)
– On se voit à quelle heure?	– What time shall we meet?
– *Disons* cinq heures.	– *Let's say* five.
Et je *dirais* même plus . . .	And I'*d* even go so far as to *say* . . .
Louis X (*dit* le Hutin)	Louis X (*called* 'the Quarrelsome')
Il n'y a plus rien *à dire*.	There's nothing more *to say*.
Comment *dit*-on en français . . ?	How do you *say* in French . . ?
Cela te *dit* d'aller au cinéma?	Do you *feel like* going to the movies/cinema?
– Ça te *dit* quelque chose, cette adresse?	– Does that address *mean* anything to you?
– Non, ça ne me *dit* rien.	– No, it doesn't *ring a bell*.

Irregular **-re** verb

IMPERATIVE

écris! (tu)   écrivez! (vous)   écrivons! (nous)

PRESENT

j'écris

tu écris

il/elle écrit

on écrit

nous écrivons

vous écrivez

ils/elles écrivent

PERFECT

j'ai écrit

tu as écrit

il/elle a écrit

on a écrit

nous avons écrit

vous avez écrit

ils/elles ont écrit

IMPERFECT

j'écrivais

tu écrivais

il/elle écrivait

on écrivait

nous écrivions

vous écriviez

ils/elles écrivaient

SIMPLE PAST

j'écrivis

tu écrivis

il/elle écrivit

on écrivit

nous écrivîmes

nous écrivîtes

ils/elles écrivirent

Similar verbs

circonscrire	contain; confine
décrire	describe
inscrire	note down; write down
prescrire	prescribe; stipulate
proscrire	ban; prohibit
récrire	write down again
réinscrire	reinscribe; reregister
retranscrire	retranscribe
souscrire	subscribe
transcrire	copy out; transcribe; transliterate

PRESENT PARTICIPLE	*PAST PARTICIPLE*
écrivant	écrit

PAST PERFECT	*PAST ANTERIOR*
j'avais écrit	j'eus écrit

FUTURE	*FUTURE PERFECT*
j'écrirai	j'aurai écrit

CONDITIONAL	*CONDITIONAL PERFECT*
j'écrirais	j'aurais écrit

PRESENT SUBJUNCTIVE	*PERFECT SUBJUNCTIVE*
que j'écrive	que j'aie écrit

IMPERFECT SUBJUNCTIVE	*PLUPERFECT SUBJUNCTIVE*
que j'écrivisse	que j'eusse écrit

Écris-moi vite.	*Write* soon.
Je lui *ai écrit* la semaine dernière.	I *wrote* to him last week.
Il faut que j'*écrive* une lettre.	I *must write* a letter.
Décrivez les voleurs.	*Describe* the thieves.
Ne pas dépasser la dose *prescrite.*	Do not exceed the *recommended* dose.

Irregular **-re** verb

IMPERATIVE
fais! (tu)   faites! (vous)   faisons! (nous)

PRESENT
je fais
tu fais
il/elle fait
on fait
nous faisons
vous faites
ils/elles font

PERFECT
j'ai fait
tu as fait
il/elle a fait
on a fait
nous avons fait
vous avez fait
ils/elles ont fait

IMPERFECT
je faisais
tu faisais
il/elle faisait
on faisait
nous faisions
vous faisiez
ils/elles faisaient

SIMPLE PAST
je fis
tu fis
il/elle fit
on fit
nous fîmes
vous fîtes
ils/elles firent

Similar verbs

contrefaire	imitate; mimic
défaire	dismantle
méfaire	damage; ravage
redéfaire	undo/take off/unpick again
refaire	redo
satisfaire	satisfy
surfaire	overrate; overprice

Que *fais*-tu?	What *are* you *doing?*
Je *fais* mes devoirs.	I'*m doing* my homework.
Il *fait* la vaisselle tous les jours.	He *does* the dishwashing every day.
J'aime *faire du cheval*.	I like *horse-riding*.
***Faites* le plein!**	*Fill* up the tank!

PRESENT PARTICIPLE faisant	*PAST PARTICIPLE* fait

PAST PERFECT j'avais fait	*PAST ANTERIOR* j'eus fait
FUTURE je ferai	*FUTURE PERFECT* j'aurai fait
CONDITIONAL je ferais	*CONDITIONAL PERFECT* j'aurais fait
PRESENT SUBJUNCTIVE que je fasse	*PERFECT SUBJUNCTIVE* que j'aie fait
IMPERFECT SUBJUNCTIVE que je fisse	*PLUPERFECT SUBJUNCTIVE* que j'eusse fait

Il *fait* chaud.	It's hot (weather).
Quel temps *a*-t-il *fait* hier?	What *was* the weather like yesterday?
Tous les matins on *faisait* une promenade ensemble.	Every morning we *used to* go for a walk together.
Que *feriez*-vous si votre père vendait la maison?	What *would you do* if your father sold the house?
Qu'est-ce tu *aurais fait* si je n'étais pas arrivé?	What *would* you *have done* if I hadn't arrived?
Je vais *faire du ski*.	I'm going *skiing*.
Que veux-tu que je *fasse?*	What do you want me to *do?*
Cela te *fera* du bien.	That *will do* you *good*.

Irregular **-re** verb

IMPERATIVE
lis! (tu) lisez! (vous) lisons! (nous)

PRESENT
je lis
tu lis
il/elle lit
on lit
nous lisons
vous lisez
ils/elles lisent

PERFECT
j'ai lu
tu as lu
il/elle a lu
on a lu
nous avons lu
vous avez lu
ils/elles ont lu

IMPERFECT
je lisais
tu lisais
il/elle lisait
on lisait
nous lisions
vous lisiez
ils/elles lisaient

SIMPLE PAST
je lus
tu lus
il/elle lut
on lut
nous lûmes
vous lûtes
ils/elles lurent

Similar verbs

élire elect
réélire re-elect
relire read again

PRESENT PARTICIPLE	PAST PARTICIPLE
lisant	lu

PAST PERFECT	PAST ANTERIOR
j'avais lu	j'eus lu

FUTURE	FUTURE PERFECT
je lirai	j'aurai lu

CONDITIONAL	CONDITIONAL PERFECT
je lirais	j'aurais lu

PRESENT SUBJUNCTIVE	PERFECT SUBJUNCTIVE
que je lise	que j'aie lu

IMPERFECT SUBJUNCTIVE	PLUPERFECT SUBJUNCTIVE
que je lusse	que j'eusse lu

Tu *as lu* le journal?	*Have* you *read* the paper?
Je *lis* beaucoup de romans policiers.	I *read* a lot of thrillers.
On l'*a élu* président.	He *was elected* president.
J'aimerais bien *relire* Le Rouge et le Noir.	I'd really like to *read* Le Rouge et le Noir *again*.
***Lisez* à haute voix . . .**	*Read* aloud . . .
Tu sais *lire*?	Can you *read*?
Alors, il alla prendre un abécédaire et je *lus* sans difficulté plusieurs pages. *La Gloire de mon père* (Marcel Pagnol)	So, he went and got an alphabet book and I *read* several pages without difficulty.

Irregular **-re** verb

IMPERATIVE
mets! (tu)   mettez! (vous)   mettons! (nous)

PRESENT	PERFECT
je *mets*	j'ai *mis*
tu *mets*	tu as *mis*
il/elle *met*	il/elle a *mis*
on *met*	on a *mis*
nous mettons	nous avons *mis*
vous mettez	vous avez *mis*
ils/elles mettent	ils/elles ont *mis*

IMPERFECT	SIMPLE PAST
je mettais	je *mis*
tu mettais	tu *mis*
il/elle mettait	il/elle *mit*
on mettait	on *mit*
nous mettions	nous *mîmes*
vous mettiez	vous *mîtes*
ils/elles mettaient	ils/elles *mirent*

Similar verbs

admettre	admit	**permettre**	allow
commettre	commit	**promettre**	promise
compromettre	compromise	**réadmettre**	readmit
démettre	dislocate	**remettre**	put again
émettre	give/send out; emit	**retransmettre**	transmit again
entremettre (s')	mediate; intervene	**sonmettre**	subject; subjugate
omettre	omit	**transmettre**	transmit

Notes   1) Italicized forms show differences from model verb 28 **vendre**.
2) **Battre** 'beat' and its compounds **combattre**, **abattre** and others are conjugated exactly as **mettre** in all forms but the past participle, which is **battu**.

PRESENT PARTICIPLE mettant	*PAST PARTICIPLE* *mis*

PAST PERFECT j'avais *mis*	*PAST ANTERIOR* j'eus *mis*
FUTURE je mettrai	*FUTURE PERFECT* j'aurai *mis*
CONDITIONAL je mettrais	*CONDITIONAL PERFECT* j'aurais *mis*
PRESENT SUBJUNCTIVE que je *mette*	*PERFECT SUBJUNCTIVE* que j'aie *mis*
IMPERFECT SUBJUNCTIVE que je *misse*	*PLUPERFECT SUBJUNCTIVE* que j'eusse *mis*

Mettez-vous à ma place!	*Put* yourself in my position!
Où *as*-tu *mis* les billets?	Where *did* you *put* the tickets?
Je te *promets* qu'on ira à Paris.	I *promise* you we'll go to Paris.
Il ne veut rien *admettre*.	He won't *admit* a thing.
On ne me *permet* pas de sortir après neuf heures.	I'm not *allowed* to go out after nine.
On ne lui *permet* pas de sortir le soir.	They don't *allow* her to go out in the evening.
Je lui *ai permis* de m'accompagner.	I *allowed* him to go with me.
Va *mettre* la table!	Go and *lay* the table!
On *se bat*!	They're *fighting*!

Irregular **-re** verb

IMPERATIVE

mouds! (tu) moulez! (vous) moulons! (nous)

PRESENT

je mouds
tu mouds
il/elle moud
on moud
nous moulons
vous moulez
ils/elles moulent

PERFECT

j'ai moulu
tu as moulu
il/elle a moulu
on a moulu
nous avons moulu
vous avez moulu
ils/elles ont moulu

IMPERFECT

je moulais
tu moulais
il/elle moulait
on moulait
nous moulions
vous mouliez
ils/elles moulaient

SIMPLE PAST

je moulus
tu moulus
il/elle moulut
on moulut
nous moulûmes
vous moulûtes
ils/elles moulurent

Similar verbs

émoudre sharpen; grind
remoudre grind again

Notes The forms are very similar to those of **coudre**, the intervening consonant being **-l-** in **moudre** (**-s-** in **coudre**).

PRESENT PARTICIPLE	*PAST PARTICIPLE*
moulant	moulu

PAST PERFECT	*PAST ANTERIOR*
j'avais moulu	j'eus moulu

FUTURE	*FUTURE PERFECT*
je moudrai	j'aurai moulu

CONDITIONAL	*CONDITIONAL PERFECT*
je moudrais	j'aurais moulu

PRESENT SUBJUNCTIVE	*PERFECT SUBJUNCTIVE*
que je moule	que j'aie moulu

IMPERFECT SUBJUNCTIVE	*PLUPERFECT SUBJUNCTIVE*
que je moulusse	que j'eusse moulu

Je vais *moudre* du café.	I'm going *to grind* some coffee.
On l'*a moulu* de coups.	They *beat* him up.
Elle *moulait* du café pour ses invités.	She *was grinding* some coffee for her guests.
Il a dit qu'*il moudrait* du café pour ce soir.	He said he *would grind* some coffee for this evening.
Je *mouds* un peu de poivre.	I'*m grinding* a little pepper.

Irregular **-re** verb

IMPERATIVE
nais! (tu)   naissez! (vous)   naissons! (nous)

PRESENT
je nais
tu nais
il/elle naît
on naît
nous naissons
vous naissez
ils/elles naissent

PERFECT
je suis né(-e)
tu es né(-e)
il est né
elle est née
on est né
nous sommes nés/nées
vous êtes né/née/nés/nées
ils sont nés
elles sont nées

IMPERFECT
je naissais
tu naissais
il/elle naissait
on naissait
nous naissions
vous naissiez
ils/elles naissaient

SIMPLE PAST
je nacquis
tu nacquis
il/elle nacquit
on nacquit
nous nacquîmes
vous nacquîtes
ils/elles nacquirent

Similar verbs

renaître   be born again; spring up again; be revived

Notes 1 This verb is not often found in the present or imperfect tenses; most often found are the perfect and simple past forms.
2 It is conjugated with **être** in compound tenses.

PRESENT PARTICIPLE	*PAST PARTICIPLE*
naissant	né

PAST PERFECT	*PAST ANTERIOR*
j'étais né(-e)	je fus né(-e)

FUTURE	*FUTURE PERFECT*
je naîtrai	je serai né(-e)

CONDITIONAL	*CONDITIONAL PERFECT*
je naîtrais	je serais né(-e)

PRESENT SUBJUNCTIVE	*PERFECT SUBJUNCTIVE*
que je naisse	que je sois né(-e)

IMPERFECT SUBJUNCTIVE	*PLUPERFECT SUBJUNCTIVE*
que je nacquisse	que je fusse né(-e)

– Quel est votre lieu de *naissance?*	– What is your place of *birth?*
– Je *suis né* à Marseille.	– I *was born* in Marseille.
Il *est né*, le divin enfant . . . (*French traditional carol*)	He *is born*, the divine child . . .
Je ne savais pas qu'il *était né* en Corse.	I didn't know he *was born* in Corsica.
Tous nos enfants *sont nés* en France.	All our children *were born* in France.

Irregular **-re** verb ending in **-indre**

IMPERATIVE
peins! (tu)   peignez! (vous)   peignons! (nous)

PRESENT
je peins
tu peins
il/elle peint
on peint
nous peignons
vous peignez
ils/elles peignent

PERFECT
j'ai peint
tu as peint
il/elle a peint
on a peint
nous avons peint
vous avez peint
ils/elles ont peint

IMPERFECT
je peignais
tu peignais
il/elle peignait
on peignait
nous peignions
vous peigniez
ils/elles peignaient

SIMPLE PAST
je peignis
tu peignis
il/elle/on peignit
on peignit
nous peignîmes
vous peignîtes
ils/elles peignirent

Similar verbs

craindre	fear
dépeindre	depict
éteindre	extinguish; put out
étreindre	embrace
plaindre	pity
(re)joindre	join (again)
repeindre	repaint

Notes **Se plaindre** 'complain', a reflexive verb (conjugated with **être** in compound tenses), follows the same pattern.

PRESENT PARTICIPLE	*PAST PARTICIPLE*
peignant	peint

PAST PERFECT	*PAST ANTERIOR*
j'avais peint	j'eus peint

FUTURE	*FUTURE PERFECT*
je peindrai	j'aurai peint

CONDITIONAL	*CONDITIONAL PERFECT*
je peindrais	j'aurais peint

PRESENT SUBJUNCTIVE	*PERFECT SUBJUNCTIVE*
que je peigne	j'aie peint

IMPERFECT SUBJUNCTIVE	*PLUPERFECT SUBJUNCTIVE*
que je peignisse	que j'eusse peint

Franchement, je le *plains*.	Quite honestly I *feel sorry for* him.
De quoi te *plains*-tu?	What are you *complaining* about?
J'*ai repeint* l'appartement.	I'*ve painted* the flat.
Monet *peignait* très souvent sa femme.	Monet often *painted* his wife.
Matisse *a peint L'Escargot*.	Matisse *painted L'Escargot*.
'Pour faire le portrait d'un oiseau *peindre* d'abord une cage avec une porte ouverte'	'To paint a portrait of a bird first *paint* a cage with an open door'
Paroles (Jacques Prévert)	

Irregular **-re** verb

IMPERATIVE
plais! (tu)   plaisez! (vous)   plaisons! (nous)

PRESENT
je plais
tu plais
il/elle plaît
on plaît
nous plaisons
vous plaisez
ils/elles plaisent

PERFECT
j'ai plu
tu as plu
il/elle a plu
on a plu
nous avons plu
vous avez plu
ils ont plu

IMPERFECT
je plaisais
tu plaisais
il/elle plasait
on plaisait
nous plaisions
vous plaisiez
ils/elles plaisaient

SIMPLE PAST
je plus
tu plus
il/elle plut
on plut
nous plûmes
vous plûtes
ils/elles plurent

Similar verbs

déplaire   displease
taire   be silent

Notes **Taire** has no accent on the third person singular present tense: **il se tait**.

PRESENT PARTICIPLE	*PAST PARTICIPLE*
plaisant	plu

PAST PERFECT	*PAST ANTERIOR*
j'avais plu	j'eus plu

FUTURE	*FUTURE PERFECT*
je plairai	j'aurai plu

CONDITIONAL	*CONDITIONAL PERFECT*
je plairais	j'aurais plu

PRESENT SUBJUNCTIVE	*PERFECT SUBJUNCTIVE*
que je plaise	que j'aie plu

IMPERFECT SUBJUNCTIVE	*PLUPERFECT SUBJUNCTIVE*
que je plusse	que j'eusse plu

S'il vous *plaît*.	*Please.*
Il me *plaît*.	I *like* him. (*lit.* he *pleases* me)
Taisez-vous, les enfants.	*Be quiet*, children.
Ils *se sont tus.*	They *fell silent.*
Ça me *plairait* beaucoup que tu viennes.	I'*d* really *like* you to come.
J'*ai essayé* de lui plaire.	I *tried* to please her.

take

Irregular **-re** verb

IMPERATIVE
prends! (tu)   prenez! (vous)   prenons! (nous)

PRESENT	*PERFECT*
je prends	j'ai pris
tu prends	tu as pris
il/elle prend	il/elle a pris
on prend	on a pris
nous prenons	nous avons pris
vous prenez	vous avez pris
ils/elles prennent	ils/elles ont pris

IMPERFECT	*SIMPLE PAST*
je prenais	je pris
tu prenais	tu pris
il/elle prenait	il/elle prit
on prenait	on prit
nous prenions	nous prîmes
vous preniez	vous prîtes
ils/elles prenaient	ils/elles prirent

Similar verbs

apprendre	learn	**entreprendre**	begin; embark upon
éprendre(s')	fall in love	**réapprendre**	relearn
comprendre	understand; consist of	**reprendre**	resume; recapture
		surprendre	surprise

Au bar:	In the bar:
Qu'est-ce que tu *prends*?	What are you *having*?
J'ai toujours mal à la tête, mais j'*ai pris* des comprimés.	I have still got a headache, but I'*ve taken* some tablets.
Où *as*-tu *appris* à nager?	Where *did* you *learn* to swim?

PRESENT PARTICIPLE prenant	*PAST PARTICIPLE* pris

PAST PERFECT
j'avais pris

PAST ANTERIOR
j'eus pris

FUTURE
je prendrai

FUTURE PERFECT
j'aurai pris

CONDITIONAL
je prendrais

CONDITIONAL PERFECT
j'aurais pris

PRESENT SUBJUNCTIVE
que je prenne
que tu prennes
qu'il/elle prenne
qu'on prenne
que nous prenions
que vous preniez
qu'ils/elles prennent

PERFECT SUBJUNCTIVE
que j'aie pris

IMPERFECT SUBJUNCTIVE
que je prisse

PLUPERFECT SUBJUNCTIVE
que j'eusse pris

Tu veux un biscuit?
Prends-en deux!

Do you want a biscuit?
Take two!

J'aime ce pull
— je le *prends.*

I like this sweater
— I'll *take* it.

Cela lui *apprendra* à vivre.

That *will teach* him a lesson.

Le service n'est pas *compris.*

Service is not *included.*

Quand il parle anglais,
personne ne le *comprend.*

When he speaks English,
no one *understands* him.

Je n'*ai* rien *compris*
— comment veux-tu que je
comprenne?

I *didn't understand* a thing
— how to you expect me to
understand?

Irregular **-re** verb

IMPERATIVE

résous! (tu)   résolvez! (vous)   résolvons! (nous)

PRESENT

je résous
tu résous
il/elle résout
on résout
nous résolvons
vous résolvez
ils/elles résolvent

IMPERFECT

je résolvais
tu résolvais
il/elle résolvait
on résolvait
nous résolvions
vous résolviez
ils/elles résolvaient

PERFECT

j'ai résolu
tu as résolu
il/elle a résolu
on a résolu
nous avons résolu
vous avez résolu
ils/elles ont résolu

SIMPLE PAST

je résolus
tu résolus
il/elle résolut
on résolut
nous résolûmes
vous résolûtes
ils/elles résolurent

Similar verbs

absoudre   absolve; pardon
dissoudre   dissolve

PRESENT PARTICIPLE résolvant	*PAST PARTICIPLE* résolu

PAST PERFECT j'avais résolu	*PAST ANTERIOR* j'eus résolu
FUTURE je résoudrai	*FUTURE PERFECT* j'aurai résolu
CONDITIONAL je résoudrais	*CONDITIONAL PERFECT* j'aurais résolu
PRESENT SUBJUNCTIVE que je résolve	*PERFECT SUBJUNCTIVE* que j'aie résolu
IMPERFECT SUBJUNCTIVE que je résolusse	*PLUPERFECT SUBJUNCTIVE* que j'eusse résolu

Il n'*a* pas *résolu* le problème.	He *hasn't solved* the problem.
Je *me suis résolu* à quitter la compagnie.	I *made up my mind* to leave the company.
Il faut faire *dissoudre* le sel dans de l'eau.	You have to *dissolve* the salt in water.
Il *a résolu* de partir.	He's *made up his mind* to leave.
L'eau *dissout* le sel.	Water *dissolves* salt.
Je vous *absous!*	I *let* you *off!*

Irregular **-re** verb

IMPERATIVE

ris! (tu)　　　　　riez! (vous)　　　　　rions! (nous)

PRESENT
je ris
tu ris
il/elle rit
on rit
nous rions
vous riez
ils/elles rient

PERFECT
j'ai ri
tu as ri
il/elle a ri
on a ri
nous avons ri
vous avez ri
ils ont ri

IMPERFECT
je riais
tu riais
il/elle riait
on riait
nous riions
vous riiez
ils/elles riaient

SIMPLE PAST
je ris
tu ris
il/elle rit
on rit
nous rîmes
vous rîtes
ils/elles rirent

Similar verbs

sourire　　　　　smile

PRESENT PARTICIPLE	*PAST PARTICIPLE*
riant	ri

PAST PERFECT	*PAST ANTERIOR*
j'avais ri	j'eus ri

FUTURE	*FUTURE PERFECT*
je rirai	j'aurai ri

CONDITIONAL	*CONDITIONAL PERFECT*
je rirais	j'aurais ri

PRESENT SUBJUNCTIVE	*PERFECT SUBJUNCTIVE*
que je rie	que j'aie ri

IMPERFECT SUBJUNCTIVE	*PLUPERFECT SUBJUNCTIVE*
que je risse	que j'eusse ri

'Tu *souriais*
Et moi je *souriais* de même'
Barbara (Jacques Prévert)

'You *were smiling*
And I *smiled* too'

Rira bien qui *rira* le dernier.

He who *laughs* last *laughs* best.

Ne *riez* pas.

Don't *laugh*.

On s'est tordu de *rire.*

We split our sides.

On *a* bien *ri.*

We *had* a good *laugh.*

Elle *riait* de lui.

She *was laughing* at him.

Tu *ris* — pourquoi?

You're *laughing* — why?

Ils *rient* aux éclats!

They're *roaring with laughter!*

Irregular **-re** verb

IMPERATIVE

suis! (tu)   suivez! (vous)   suivons! (nous)

PRESENT   *PERFECT*

je suis   j'ai suivi
tu suis   tu as suivi
il/elle suit   il/elle a suivi
on suit   on a suivi
nous suivons   nous avons suivi
vous suivez   vous avez suivi
ils/elles suivent   ils/elles ont suivi

IMPERFECT   *SIMPLE PAST*

je suivais   je suivis
tu suivais   tu suivis
il/elle suivait   il/elle suivit
on suivait   on suivit
nous suivions   nous suivîmes
vous suiviez   vous suivîtes
ils/elles suivaient   ils/elles suivirent

Similar verbs

poursuivre   pursue

Notes   1) **S'ensuivre** is also conjugated this way (using **être** in compound
          tenses).
          2) There is rarely confusion between the two meanings of **je suis** 'I
          am/I follow'; the context normally makes the sense clear.

PRESENT PARTICIPLE suivant	*PAST PARTICIPLE* suivi
PAST PERFECT j'avais suivi	*PAST ANTERIOR* j'eus suivi
FUTURE je suivrai	*FUTURE PERFECT* j'aurai suivi
CONDITIONAL je suivrais	*CONDITIONAL PERFECT* j'aurais suivi
PRESENT SUBJUNCTIVE que je suive	*PERFECT SUBJUNCTIVE* que j'aie suivi
IMPERFECT SUBJUNCTIVE que je suivisse	*PLUPERFECT SUBJUNCTIVE* que j'eusse suivi

Suivez-moi, s'il vous plaît!	*Follow* me, please.
Ce chien nous *suit* depuis une heure.	This dog *has been following* us for an hour.
La police *a poursuivi* les voleurs.	The police *pursued* the thieves
A suivre.	*To be continued.*
Il *a été poursuivi* en justice.	He *was prosecuted.*

48 traire — milk

Irregular **-re** verb

IMPERATIVE
trais! (tu)   trayez! (vous)   trayons! (nous)

PRESENT	**PERFECT**
je trais	j'ai trait
tu trais	tu as trait
il/elle trait	il/elle a trait
on trait	on a trait
nous trayons	nous avons trait
vous trayez	vous avez trait
ils/elles traient	ils/elles ont trait

IMPERFECT	**SIMPLE PAST**
je trayais	—
tu trayais	
il/elle trayait	
on trayait	
nous trayions	
vous trayiez	
ils/elles trayaient	

Similar verbs

abstraire	abstract	**retraire**	re-milk
distraire	entertain; divert	**soustraire**	subtract
extraire	extract		

PRESENT PARTICIPLE	**PAST PARTICIPLE**
trayant	trait

PAST PERFECT	**PAST ANTERIOR**
j'avais trait	j'eus trait

FUTURE	**FUTURE PERFECT**
je trairai	j'aurai trait

CONDITIONAL	**CONDITIONAL PERFECT**
je trairais	j'aurais trait

PRESENT SUBJUNCTIVE	**PERFECT SUBJUNCTIVE**
que je traie	que j'aie trait

IMPERFECT SUBJUNCTIVE	**PLUPERFECT SUBJUNCTIVE**
—	que j'eusse trait

On *trait* les vaches à cinq heures.   We *milk* the cows at five o'clock.

J'aime regarder la télé
pour me *distraire*.   I like watching TV for
entertainment.

On *extrait* le charbon ici.   They *mine* coal here.

Dans le passé on *extrayait*
le marbre.   In the past they *quarried*
marble.

Tu m'*as distrait*.   You *distracted* me.

On l'*a soustrait* à la justice.   They *shielded* him from the law.

Irregular **-re** verb

IMPERATIVE
vaincs! (tu) vainquez! (vous) vainquons! (nous)

PRESENT
je vaincs
tu vaincs
il/elle vainc
on vainc
nous vainquons
vous vainquez
ils/elles vainquent

PERFECT
j'ai vaincu
tu as vaincu
il/elle a vaincu
on a vaincu
nous avons vaincu
vous avez vaincu
ils/elles ont vaincu

IMPERFECT
je vainquais
tu vainquais
il/elle vainquait
on vainquait
nous vainquions
vous vainquiez
ils/elles vainquaient

SIMPLE PAST
je vainquis
tu vainquis
il/elle vainquit
on vainquit
nous vainquîmes
vous vainquîtes
ils/elles vainquirent

Similar verbs

convaincre convince

Notes In front of a vowel (except **-u-**) the **-c-** of **vaincre** changes to **-qu-**.

PRESENT PARTICIPLE	PAST PARTICIPLE
vainquant	vaincu

PAST PERFECT	PAST ANTERIOR
j'avais vaincu	j'eus vaincu

FUTURE	FUTURE PERFECT
je vaincrai	j'aurai vaincu

CONDITIONAL	CONDITIONAL PERFECT
je vaincrais	j'aurais vaincu

PRESENT SUBJUNCTIVE	PERFECT SUBJUNCTIVE
que je vainque	que j'aie vaincu

IMPERFECT SUBJUNCTIVE	PLUPERFECT SUBJUNCTIVE
que je vainquisse	que j'eusse vaincu

Il m'*a convaincu* d'abandonner le projet.	He *convinced* me to give up the project.
Nous *avons vaincu!*	We *won!*
Je ne *suis* pas *convaincu.*	I'*m* not *convinced.*
Nous *vaincrons!*	We *shall win!*
Il *va vaincre* la maladie.	He *will overcome* the illness.
Il *était vaincu* d'avance.	He *was defeated* before he started.
Wellington *vainquit* à Waterloo.	Wellington *won* at Waterloo.

Irregular **-re** verb

IMPERATIVE

vis! (tu)   vivez! (vous)   vivons! (nous)

PRESENT

je vis
tu vis
il/elle vit
on vit
nous vivons
vous vivez
ils/elles vivent

PERFECT

j'ai vécu
tu as vécu
il/elle a vécu
on a vécu
nous avons vécu
vous avez vécu
ils/elles ont vécu

IMPERFECT

je vivais
tu vivais
il/elle vivait
on vivait
nous vivions
vous viviez
ils/elles vivaient

SIMPLE PAST

je vécus
tu vécus
il/elle vécut
on vécut
nous vécûmes
vous vécûtes
ils/elles vécurent

Similar verbs

revivre   live again
survivre   survive

PRESENT PARTICIPLE vivant	*PAST PARTICIPLE* vécu

PAST PERFECT j'avais vécu	*PAST ANTERIOR* j'eus vécu
FUTURE je vivrai	*FUTURE PERFECT* j'aurai vécu
CONDITIONAL je vivrais	*CONDITIONAL PERFECT* j'aurais vécu
PRESENT SUBJUNCTIVE que je vive	*PERFECT SUBJUNCTIVE* que j'aie vécu
IMPERFECT SUBJUNCTIVE que je vécusse	*PLUPERFECT SUBJUNCTIVE* que j'eusse vécu

Tant que je *vivrai* . . .	As long as I *live* . . .
Il *a vécu* à Rome.	He *lived* in Rome.
En 1883 Gauguin *vivait* à Paris	In 1883 Gauguin *was living* in Paris.
On a juste de quoi *vivre.*	We have just enough *to live* on.
Nous *vivons* chez nos parents.	We *live* at our parents' house.
Pétrarque *vécut* en Provence.	Petrarch *lived* in Provence.
Ils n'*avaient* jamais *vécu* à Paris.	They *had* never *lived* in Paris.
Je ne crois pas qu'il *vivra* très longtemps.	I don't think he'*ll live* long.

Irregular reflexive verb in **-oir**

IMPERATIVE
assieds-toi! (tu)   asseyez-vous! (vous)   asseyons-nous (nous)

PRESENT
je m'assieds (m'assois)
tu t'assieds (t'assois)
il/elle s'assied (s'assoit)
on s'assied (s'assoit)
nous nous asseyons
vous vous asseyez
ils/elles s'asseyent (assoient)

PERFECT
je me suis assis(-e)
tu t'es assis(-e)
il s'est assis
elle s'est assise
on s'est assis
nous nous sommes assis(-es)
vous vous êtes assis(-e)(-es)
ils se sont assis
elles se sont assises

IMPERFECT
je m'asseyais
tu t'asseyais
il/elle s'asseyait
on s'asseyait
nous nous asseyions
vous vous asseyiez
ils/elles s'asseyaient

SIMPLE PAST
je m'assis
tu t'assis
il/elle s'assit
on s'assit
nous nous assîmes
vous vous assîtes
ils/elles s'assirent

Notes   This verb is the only one of its kind. Where two forms exist, the first is more common; those with **-oi-** are much less common.

PRESENT PARTICIPLE	PAST PARTICIPLE
asseyant/assoyant	assis

PAST PERFECT	PAST ANTERIOR
je m'étais assis(-e)	je me fus assis(-e)

FUTURE	FUTURE PERFECT
je m'assiérai or	je me serai assis(-e)
je m'assoirai	

CONDITIONAL	CONDITIONAL PERFECT
je m'assiérais or	je me serais assis(-e)
je m'assoirais	

PRESENT SUBJUNCTIVE	PERFECT SUBJUNCTIVE
que je m'asseye or	que je me sois assis(-e)
que je m'assoie	

IMPERFECT SUBJUNCTIVE	PLUPERFECT SUBJUNCTIVE
que je m'assisse	que je me fusse assis(-e)

'. . . les uns se lèvent quand les autres s'agenouillent, *s'asseyent* quand les autres sont debout . . .' *Lettres de mon moulin* *(Les Trois Messes basses)* (Alphonse Daudet)	'. . . some stand up when others kneel down, *sit down* when others are standing . . .'
Asseyez-vous, les enfants.	*Sit down*, children.
Je *me suis assis* devant lui.	I *sat down* in front of him.
Où voulez-vous *vous asseoir?*	Where do you want to *sit?*

Irregular modal verb in **-oir**

IMPERATIVE

dois! (tu)   devez! (vous)   devons! (nous)

PRESENT	**PERFECT**
je dois	j'ai dû
tu dois	tu as dû
il/elle doit	il/elle a dû
on doit	on a dû
nous devons	nous avons dû
vous devez	vous avez dû
ils/elles doivent	ils/elles ont dû

IMPERFECT	**SIMPLE PAST**
je devais	je dus
tu devais	tu dus
il/elle devait	il/elle dut
on devait	on dut
nous devions	nous dûmes
vous deviez	vous dûtes
ils/elles devaient	ils/elles durent

Notes   1) The imperative is rarely found.
2) If the past participle requires a feminine agreement the spelling is **due.**
3) As a full verb, **devoir** means to owe.
4) It is the only verb of its type, though similarities with **pouvoir** and **vouloir** will be obvious (➤model verbs *55, 61*).

Examples of use as a full verb:

Je lui *dois* 50 francs.   I *owe* her 50 francs.

Il me *devait* un million de francs.   He *owed* me a million francs

PRESENT PARTICIPLE	*PAST PARTICIPLE*
devant	dû

PAST PERFECT	*PAST ANTERIOR*
j'avais dû	j'eus dû

FUTURE
je devrai

FUTURE PERFECT
j'aurai dû

CONDITIONAL
je devrais

CONDITIONAL PERFECT
j'aurais dû

PRESENT SUBJUNCTIVE
que je doive

PERFECT SUBJUNCTIVE
que j'aie dû

IMPERFECT SUBJUNCTIVE
que je dusse

PLUPERFECT SUBJUNCTIVE
que j'eusse dû

Examples of use as a modal verb:

Tu *dois* y arriver avant huit heures.	You *must* get there by eight o'clock.
On *doit* écouter les instructions.	We *must* listen to the instructions.
On *devra* partir à l'aube.	We'*ll* have to leave at dawn.
Il *a dû* travailler jusqu'à minuit.	He *had to* work until midnight.
Il *a dû* avoir un accident.	He *must have* had an accident.
Elle *devait* l'accompagner en vacances.	She *was meant* to go on vacation with him.
On *devrait* téléphoner tout de suite.	Someone *ought to* phone immediately.
Tu *aurais dû* lui offrir des fleurs.	You *ought to have* given her some flowers.

Irregular impersonal modal verb in **-oir**

IMPERATIVE
—

PRESENT	*PERFECT*
il faut	il a fallu

IMPERFECT	*SIMPLE PAST*
il fallait	il fallut

Notes 1) This verb only exists in the third person singular, and covers meanings from 'it is necessary', 'one must' to 'we have to', 'you have to'.
2) **'Il me faut'** = I need. (The addition of the personal indirect object pronoun personalizes the meaning.)

Il *faut* appeler les pompiers.	We *must* call the fire department/brigade.
Il *faut* arriver à l'heure.	You *must* arrive on time.
Il *faut* que j'arrive à l'heure.	I *must* arrive on time.
Il *a fallu* nettoyer la maison.	We *had to* clean the house (and we did).
Il *faudrait* acheter du pain.	We *ought to* buy some bread.

PRESENT PARTICIPLE	PAST PARTICIPLE
—	fallu

PAST PERFECT	PAST ANTERIOR
il avait fallu	il eut fallu

FUTURE	FUTURE PERFECT
il faudra	il aura fallu

CONDITIONAL	CONDITIONAL PERFECT
il faudrait	il aurait fallu

PRESENT SUBJUNCTIVE	PERFECT SUBJUNCTIVE
qu'il faille	qu'il ait fallu

IMPERFECT SUBJUNCTIVE	PLUPERFECT SUBJUNCTIVE
qu'il fallût	qu'il eut fallu

Si Dieu n'existait pas, il *faudrait* **l'inventer.** (Voltaire)	If God did not exist, we *should have* to invent Him.
Il me *faut* **des oeufs.**	I *need* some eggs.
Il ne *faut* **pas courir!**	*No* running!
Il ne *faut* **jamais nager seul.**	One/You *should* never swim alone.
Il *aurait fallu* **téléphoner plus tôt.**	Someone *ought to have* phoned earlier.
Il *fallut* **signer l'Armistice en juin 1940.**	It *was necessary* to sign the Armistice in June 1940.

Irregular impersonal verb in **-oir**

IMPERATIVE

—

PRESENT
il pleut

PERFECT
il a plu

IMPERFECT
il pleuvait

SIMPLE PAST
il plut

Notes   1) This impersonal verb is normally only found in the third person singular. Occasionally a figurative usage may give rise to a plural verb. Example: **Les coups de fusil pleuvent sur les hommes** 'The gun shots rained on the men'.
2) There are no other verbs like it.

PRESENT PARTICIPLE pleuvant	*PAST PARTICIPLE* plu

PAST PERFECT il avait plu	*PAST ANTERIOR* il eut plu
FUTURE il pleuvra	*FUTURE PERFECT* il aura plu
CONDITIONAL il pleuvrait	*CONDITIONAL PERFECT* il aurait plu
PRESENT SUBJUNCTIVE qu'il pleuve	*PERFECT SUBJUNCTIVE* qu'il ait plu
IMPERFECT SUBJUNCTIVE qu'il plût	*PLUPERFECT SUBJUNCTIVE* qu'il eût plu

Il *pleut.*	It's *raining.*
Il va *pleuvoir.*	It's going *to rain.*
Il a *plu* hier.	It *rained* yesterday.
J'espère qu'il ne *pleuvra* pas au mois de juillet.	I hope it *won't rain* in July.
Il *pleuvait* toute la journée.	It *was raining* all day long.
Il a dit qu'il *pleuvrait.*	He said it *would rain.*
Elle m'a dit qu'il *avait plu* longtemps.	She told me it *had rained* for a long time.

Irregular modal verb in **-oir**

IMPERATIVE

—

PRESENT

je peux/je puis
tu peux
il/elle peut
on peut
nous pouvons
vous pouvez
ils/elles peuvent

PERFECT

j'ai pu
tu as pu
il/elle a pu
on a pu
nous avons pu
vous avez pu
ils/elles ont pu

IMPERFECT

je pouvais
tu pouvais
il/elle pouvait
on pouvait
nous pouvions
vous pouviez
ils/elles pouvaient

SIMPLE PAST

je pus
tu pus
il/elle put
on put
nous pûmes
vous pûtes
ils/elles purent

Notes   1) There are no other verbs like **pouvoir**, though similarities with **vouloir** and **devoir** will be evident (➤model verbs 61 and 52 respectively).
2) The various tenses of **pouvoir** convey a full variety of meanings.
3) **Puis-je...** for 'May I...' is going out of use and is considered old-fashioned.

PRESENT PARTICIPLE pouvant	*PAST PARTICIPLE* pu

PAST PERFECT j'avais pu	*PAST ANTERIOR* j'eus pu
FUTURE je pourrai	*FUTURE PERFECT* j'aurai pu
CONDITIONAL je pourrais	*CONDITIONAL PERFECT* j'aurais pu
PRESENT SUBJUNCTIVE que je puisse que nous puissions	*PERFECT SUBJUNCTIVE* que j'aie pu
IMPERFECT SUBJUNCTIVE que je pusse	*PLUPERFECT SUBJUNCTIVE* que j'eusse pu

Je *peux* entrer?	*May* I come in?
Il ne *peut* pas fermer cette fenêtre.	He *can*'t close that window.
On *peut* aller à la patinoire.	We *can* go to the ice-rink.
On *pourra* y aller en voiture.	We'*ll be able to* go there by car.
Il *pourrait* pleuvoir plus tard.	It *might* rain later.
Pourriez-vous me passer le sel?	*Could* you pass me the salt?
À l'époque on *pouvait* y acheter toutes sortes de choses.	At the time you *could* buy all sorts of things there.
Tu *aurais pu* me le dire!	You *could have* told me!
J'*ai pu* réparer la serrure.	I'*ve managed* to fix the lock.
Je regrette qu'on ne *puisse* plus y aller.	I'm sorry you *can*'t go there any more.

Irregular verb in **-oir**

IMPERATIVE
promeus! (tu)   promouvez! (vous)   promouvons! (nous)

PRESENT
je promeus
tu promeus
il/elle promeut
on promeut
nous promouvons
vous promouvez
ils/elles promeuvent

PERFECT
j'ai promu
tu as promu
il/elle a promu
on a promu
nous avons promu
vous avez promu
ils/elles ont promu

IMPERFECT
je promouvais
tu promouvais
il/elle promouvait
on promouvait
nous promouvions
vous promouviez
ils promouvaient

SIMPLE PAST
je promus
tu promus
il/elle promut
on promut
nous promûmes
vous promûtes
ils promurent

Similar verbs

émouvoir   affect; disturb; arouse
mouvoir   move

Notes   **Promouvoir** is found most frequently in compound tenses, and in the infinitive and compound tenses.

PRESENT PARTICIPLE	PAST PARTICIPLE
promouvant	promu

PAST PERFECT	PAST ANTERIOR
j'avais promu	j'eus promu

FUTURE	FUTURE PERFECT
je promouvrai	j'aurai promu

CONDITIONAL	CONDITIONAL PERFECT
je promouvrais	j'aurais promu

PRESENT SUBJUNCTIVE	PERFECT SUBJUNCTIVE
que je promeuve	que j'aie promu

IMPERFECT SUBJUNCTIVE	PLUPERFECT SUBJUNCTIVE
que je promusse	que j'eusse promu

On m'*a promu*.	I*'ve* been *promoted.*
Il faut *promouvoir* l'étude des langues vivantes.	It's necessary to *encourage* the study of modern languages.
Je *suis ému*.	I *am overcome.* (*With emotion*)
Cette musique m'*a* toujours *ému.*	This music *has* always *moved* me.
La misère de ces pauvres gens l'*émouvait* profondément.	The poverty of those poor folk *moved* him deeply.
Les événements de Mai 68 *émurent* profondément. les Français.	The events of May '68 deeply *troubled* the French.

Irregular **-oir** verb ending in **-cevoir**

IMPERATIVE
reçois! (tu)   recevez! (vous)   recevons! (nous)

PRESENT
je reçois
tu reçois
il/elle reçoit
on reçoit
nous recevons
vous recevez
ils/elles reçoivent

PERFECT
j'ai reçu
tu as reçu
il/elle a reçu
on a reçu
nous avons reçu
vous avez reçu
ils/elles ont reçu

IMPERFECT
je recevais
tu recevais
il/elle recevait
on recevait
nous recevions
vous receviez
ils/elles recevaient

SIMPLE PAST
je reçus
tu reçus
il/elle reçut
on reçut
nous reçûmes
vous reçûtes
ils/elles reçurent

Similar verbs

apercevoir   notice; see   **concevoir**   imagine; conceive
décevoir   deceive; disappoint   **percevoir**   perceive; detect; make out

Notes   As usual the cedilla is required whenever **c** precedes **o** or **u**.

PRESENT PARTICIPLE
recevant

PAST PARTICIPLE
reçu

PAST PERFECT
j'avais reçu

PAST ANTERIOR
j'eus reçu

FUTURE
je recevrai

FUTURE PERFECT
j'aurai reçu

CONDITIONAL
je recevrais

CONDITIONAL PERFECT
j'aurais reçu

PRESENT SUBJUNCTIVE
que je reçoive
qu'ils/elles reçoivent

PERFECT SUBJUNCTIVE
que j'aie reçu

IMPERFECT SUBJUNCTIVE
que je reçusse

PLUPERFECT SUBJUNCTIVE
que j'eusse reçu

Le courier

- Tous les matins je *reçois* au moins trois factures.

- Qu'est-ce que vous *avez reçu* ce matin?

- Rien! Mais je n'*ai* pas encore *aperçu* le facteur.

Tu *recevras* ma lettre demain.

Tu l'*aurais reçue* ce matin si je l'avais postée en ville.

On *a reçu* le maire.

D'ici on *aperçoit* le sommet de la montagne.

The mail

– Every morning I *receive* at least three bills.

– What *have* you *received* this morning?

– Nothing! But I *have*n't yet *caught sight of* the mailman/postman.

You'*ll receive* my letter tomorrow.

You *would have received* it this morning if I'd posted it in town.

They *entertained* the mayor.

From here you *can* just *glimpse* the mountain top.

Irregular modal verb in **-oir**

IMPERATIVE
sache! (tu)   sachez! (vous)   sachons! (nous)

PRESENT	**PERFECT**
je sais	j'ai su
tu sais	tu as su
il/elle sait	il/elle a su
on sait	on a su
nous savons	nous avons su
vous savez	vous avez su
ils/elles savent	ils/elles ont su

IMPERFECT	**SIMPLE PAST**
je savais	je sus
tu savais	tu sus
il/elle savait	il/elle sut
on savait	on sut
nous savions	nous sûmes
vous saviez	vous sûtes
ils/elles savaient	ils/elles surent

Note   1) This verb is important in two areas: (i) it is used for knowing a fact; (ii) it also has the meaning of 'to be able', in the sense of having acquired a skill.
2) It should not be used for knowing people, countries, or works of art, music, theatre, literature etc., where the correct verb is **connaître** (➤model verb 32).

Examples of use as a full verb:

– **Quelle heure est-il?**	– What time is it?
– **Je ne *sais* pas.**	– I don't *know*.
Je ne *savais* pas qu'il était à New York.	I didn't *know* he was in New York.
Je ne veux pas qu'on *sache* mon nom.	I don't want anyone to *know* my name.
Il *a su* son nom.	He *found out* her name.

PRESENT PARTICIPLE	**PAST PARTICIPLE**
sachant	su

PAST PERFECT	**PAST ANTERIOR**
j'avais su	j'eus su

FUTURE
je saurai

FUTURE PERFECT
j'aurai su

CONDITIONAL
je saurais

CONDITIONAL PERFECT
j'aurais su

PRESENT SUBJUNCTIVE
que je sache
que nous sachions

PERFECT SUBJUNCTIVE
que j'aie su

IMPERFECT SUBJUNCTIVE
que je susse

PLUPERFECT SUBJUNCTIVE
que j'eusse su

Examples of use as a full verb:

On ne *sait* jamais.	You never *know*.
Il *saura* les détails demain.	He'*ll know* the details tomorrow.
Finalement, on *sut* que Dreyfus était innocent.	In the end, people *learnt* that Dreyfus was innocent.
Il m'a dit qu'il n'*avait* pas *su* le numéro de la maison.	He told me he *had*n't *known* the house number.

Example of use as a modal verb:

Je ne *saurais* pas le dire.	I *could*n't say.
Tu *sais* jouer du piano?	*Can* you play the piano?
Vous *savez* nager?	*Can* you swim?
A cette époque je ne *savais* pas jouer du violon.	At that time I *could*n't play the violin.

Irregular verb in **-oir**

IMPERATIVE
vaux! (tu)   valez! (vous)   valons! (nous)

PRESENT
je vaux
tu vaux
il/elle vaut
on vaut
nous valons
vous valez
ils/elles valent

PERFECT
j'ai valu
tu as valu
il/elle a valu
on a valu
nous avons valu
vous avez valu
ils/elles ont valu

IMPERFECT
je valais
tu valais
il/elle valait
on valait
nous valions
vous valiez
ils/elles valaient

SIMPLE PAST
je valus
tu valus
il/elle valut
on valut
nous valûmes
vous valûtes
ils/elles valurent

Similar verbs

équivaloir   be equivalent; amount to
prévaloir   prevail
revaloir   pay back

Notes   Impersonal usage: **il vaut mieux** 'it is better'.

PRESENT PARTICIPLE	PAST PARTICIPLE
valant	valu

PAST PERFECT
j'avais valu

PAST ANTERIOR
j'eus valu

FUTURE
ja vaudrai

FUTURE PERFECT
j'aurai valu

CONDITIONAL
je vaudrais

CONDITIONAL PERFECT
j'aurais valu

PRESENT SUBJUNCTIVE
que je vaille
que tu vailles
qu'il/elle vaille
qu'on vaille
que nous valions
que vous valiez
qu'ils/elles vaillent

PERFECT SUBJUNCTIVE
que je'aie valu

IMPERFECT SUBJUNCTIVE
que je valusse

PLUPERFECT SUBJUNCTIVE
que j'eusse valu

Ça *vaut* combien?	How much is that *worth*?
Ce tableau *vaut* un million.	That painting is *worth* a million.
Ce film *vaut* la peine d'être vu.	That movie is *worth* seeing.
Ce type ne *vaut* pas cher.	That guy's not much *good*.
Ce café ne *vaut* pas le brésilien.	This coffee's not *as good* as the Brazilian.
Cette affaire lui *a valu* bien des soucis.	That affair *brought* him a lot of worry.
Il *vaut mieux* partir.	It's *better* to leave.
Il *vaudrait mieux* partir tout de suite.	It *would be better* to leave at once.

60 voir
see

Irregular verb in **-oir**

IMPERATIVE
vois! (tu)   voyez! (vous)   voyons! (nous)

PRESENT
je vois
tu vois
il/elle voit
on voit
nous voyons
vous voyez
ils voient

PERFECT
j'ai vu
tu as vu
il/elle a vu
on a vu
nous avons vu
vous avez vu
ils ont vu

IMPERFECT
je voyais
tu voyais
il/elle voyait
on voyait
nous voyions
vous voyiez
ils/elles voyaient

SIMPLE PAST
je vis
tu vis
il/elle vit
on vit
nous vîmes
vous vîtes
ils/elles virent

Similar verbs
entrevoir   glimpse
prévoir   foresee; predict
revoir   see again

Notes   1) The future and conditional tenses of **prévoir** are **je prévoirai** and **je prévoirais** respectively.
2) **Pourvoir** (to provide) is also similarly conjugated: **je pourvoirai** in the future tense; **je pourvoirais** in the conditional; and **je pourvus** in the simple past, **que je pourvusse** in the imperfect subjunctive.

PRESENT PARTICIPLE	PAST PARTICIPLE
voyant	vu

PAST PERFECT
j'avais vu

PAST ANTERIOR
j'eus vu

FUTURE
je verrai

FUTURE PERFECT
j'aurai vu

CONDITIONAL
je verrais

CONDITIONAL PERFECT
j'aurais vu

PRESENT SUBJUNCTIVE
que je voie

PERFECT SUBJUNCTIVE
que j'aie vu

IMPERFECT SUBJUNCTIVE
que je visse

PLUPERFECT SUBJUNCTIVE
que j'eusse vu

Devant le cinéma

– Tu *as vu* ce film?

– Non. Je vais le *voir* demain.

Outside the cinema

– *Have* you *seen* that film?

– No, I'm going to *see* it tomorrow.

A la maison

– Je n'ai pas encore nettoyé la cuisine.

– Ça *se voit!*

At home

– I haven't cleaned the kitchen yet.

– That's *obvious!*

Au musée

– Je suis désolée que vous n'*ayez* pas *vu* l'exposition d'art breton.

– Ça ne fait rien! On la *verra* à Paris.

At the museum

– I'm so sorry you *didn't see* the Breton art exhibition.

– Never mind. We'*ll see it* in Paris.

61 vouloir   want

Irregular modal verb in **-oir**

IMPERATIVE

veuille! (tu)   veuillez! (vous)   voulons! (nous)

PRESENT	**PERFECT**
je veux	j'ai voulu
tu veux	tu as voulu
il/elle veut	il/elle a voulu
on veut	on a voulu
nous voulons	nous avons voulu
vous voulez	vous avez voulu
ils/elles veulent	ils/elles ont voulu

IMPERFECT	**SIMPLE PAST**
je voulais	je voulus
tu voulais	tu voulus
il/elle voulait	il/elle voulut
on voulait	on voulut
nous voulions	nous voulûmes
vous vouliez	vous voulûtes
ils/elles voulaient	ils/elles voulurent

Notes   1) This is the only verb of its type, though the patterns of **pouvoir** and **devoir** are similar (➤model verbs 55, 52). Notice that the present indicative tense has irregular forms in the singular and the 3rd person plural, while the 1st and 2nd persons plural have the stem of the infinitive.

2) The imperative is used as a courtesy in such phrases as **Veuillez agréer, monsieur, l'expression de mes sentiments distingués** (Yours faithfully); **Veuillez répondre tout de suite** (Please be so good as to reply immediately).

3) Used transitively, **vouloir** means 'to want (something)'.

Examples of use as a full verb:

Tu *veux* une glace?   *Do* you *want* an ice-cream?

Je *voudrais* cinq kilos de pommes de terre.   I'd *like* 5 kilos of potatoes.

PRESENT PARTICIPLE	PAST PARTICIPLE
voulant	voulu

PAST PERFECT	PAST ANTERIOR
j'avais voulu	j'eus voulu

FUTURE	FUTURE PERFECT
je voudrai	j'aurai voulu

CONDITIONAL	CONDITIONAL PERFECT
je voudrais	j'aurais voulu

PRESENT SUBJUNCTIVE	PERFECT SUBJUNCTIVE
que je veuille	que j'aie voulu
que nous voulions	

IMPERFECT SUBJUNCTIVE	PLUPERFECT SUBJUNCTIVE
que je voulusse	que j'eusse voulu

Examples of use as a modal verb:

Je *veux* regarder ce film.	I *want* to watch that film.
Il ne *veut* pas aller en Espagne.	He *doesn't want* to go to Spain.
Voulez-vous vérifier la pression des pneus?	*Will* you check the tire/tyre pressure?
Voulez-vous me téléphoner ce soir?	*Will* you phone me this evening?
Je *voudrais* voir le chef de personnel.	I*'d like* to see the personnel manager.
Elle ne *veut* rien faire.	She *won't* do a thing.
J'*aurais voulu* assister à leur mariage.	I *would have liked* to go to their wedding.
Jules César *voulut* envahir la Bretange.	Julius Caesar *wanted* to invade Britain (and did so).

C
SUBJECT INDEX

Subject

Paragraph

(Section A 'Verbs in French: their functions and uses')

D
VERB INDEX

Verb index

There are over 2,000 entries in the Verb index.

Each verb, or verbal expression, is given in French, with its English meaning, a note as to whether it is transitive (tr), intransitive (intr), or reflexive (ref), and its conjugation group.

Verbs which are set out in the Model French Verbs section are noted ⊡.

The 13 verbs and their compounds which are conjugated with **être** in compound tenses are marked * after the conjugation number. Reflexive verbs are not thus marked, as all reflexive verbs are conjugated with **être** in compound tenses.

Verbs which begin with **h-** are marked *h if they require no liaison (aspirate h).

Abbreviations: **qch** – quelque chose; **qqn** – quelqu'un

A

abandonner (tr)	give up, abandon 7
abasourdir (tr)	dumbfound, bewilder 16
abattre (tr)	slaughter 39
abîmer (tr)	spoil 7
abolir (tr)	abolish 16
abonder (intr)	be abundant, abound 7
abonner, s' (ref)	subscribe 7
aborder (tr)	reach, approach 7
aboutir (intr)	work out well 16
aboutir à (intr)	result in 16
aboyer (intr)	bark 12
abriter (tr)	shelter (someone) 7
abriter, s' (ref)	take shelter 7
absenter, s' (ref)	be absent, absent oneself 7
absorber (tr)	take over, absorb 7
absoudre (tr)	absolve 45
abstenir de, s' (ref)	keep off, abstain/ refrain from 26
abuser de (intr)	misuse 7
accélérer (tr & intr)	accelerate 13
accepter (tr)	agree to, accept 7
accommoder de qch. s' (ref)	make the best of 7
accompagner (tr)	accompany 7
accomplir (tr)	fulfil, achieve 16

accorder (tr)	grant (request), tune (instrument) 7
accorder avec, s' (ref)	accord with 7
accoster (tr)	accost 7
accoucher de (intr)	give birth to 7
accouder, s' (ref)	lean (on elbows) 7
accoupler (tr)	couple 7
accoupler, s' (ref)	mate 7
accourir (vers/jusqu'a)(intr)	run to 19
accrocher (tr)	hook, hang up 7
accrocher à, s' (ref)	cling to 7
accroupir, s' (ref)	squat, crouch 16
accumuler (tr)	accumulate 7
accuser réception de (tr)	acknowledge (receipt of) 7
accuser (de) (tr)	accuse, charge (with crime) 7
acheter (tr)	buy, purchase 10 [M]
acquérir (tr)	acquire, get 17 [M]
acquitter (tr)	acquit 7
adapter (tr)	adapt 7
additionner (tr)	add up 7
adhérer (intr)	adhere, stick to, join 11
admettre (tr)	admit, grant to be true 39
administrer (tr)	administer 7
administrer un médicament (tr)	dose 7
admirer (tr)	admire 7
adonner à, s' (ref)	become addicted 7
adopter (tr)	adopt 7
adorer (tr)	worship, adore 7
adosser à, s' (ref)	lean up against 7
adresser (tr)	address 7
adresser à, s' (ref)	address 7
aérer (tr)	air 11
affaiblir, s' (ref)	weaken 16
affairer, s' (ref)	bustle 7
affecter (tr)	affect 7
affirmer (tr)	affirm 7
affliger (tr)	afflict, distress 13
affranchir (tr)	frank (letters) 16
affréter (tr)	charter (plane) 11
affronter (tr)	stand up to 7
agenouiller, s' (ref)	kneel (down) 7
aggraver, s' (ref)	get worse 7
agir (intr)	act, take action 16
agir de, s' (ref)	be a matter of, be about 16
il s'agit d'un homme qui . . .	*it's about a man who . . .*

allonger (tr & intr)	stretch, lengthen 13
allonger, s' (ref)	to get longer 13
allonger la sauce (tr)	thin sauce, 'spin it out' 13
allouer (tr)	allow, allocate (funds) 7
allumer (tr)	switch on, ignite, strike match 7
allumer, s' (ref)	light up, come on (lights) 7
alterner (tr)	alternate 7
amarrer (tr)	moor (boat) 7
amasser (tr)	hoard 7
améliorer (tr)	improve, upgrade 7
amender (tr)	amend 7
amortir (tr)	deaden 16
amplifier (tr)	amplify 7
amputer (tr)	amputate, cut off 7
amuser (tr)	amuse 7
amuser, s' (ref)	play around, have fun, enjoy oneself 7
analyser (tr)	analyze 7
anéantir (tr)	annihilate 16
anesthésier (tr)	anesthetize 7
animer (tr)	animate 7
annexer (tr)	annex 7
annoncer (tr)	announce 14
annuler (tr)	annul, call off, cancel 7
anticiper (tr)	anticipate 7
apercevoir (tr)	sight, spot 57
apercevoir de, s' (ref)	glimpse, notice 57
aplanir (tr)	flatten 16
apparaître (intr)	appear 32
appartenir (intr)	belong 26
appeler (tr)	call, ring up 9 [M]
appeler par radio (tr)	radio 9
appeler sous les drapeaux (tr)	call up (for military service) 9
appeler, s' (ref)	be called 9
applaudir (tr)	clap, applaud 16
appliquer (tr)	apply 7
apporter (tr)	bring 7
apprécier (tr)	enjoy, value 7
apprendre (tr)	learn 44
apprendre par coeur (tr)	learn by heart 44
apprivoiser (tr)	tame 7
approcher (tr & intr)	close in, bring close 7
approcher, s' (ref)	approach 7
approfondir (tr)	deepen 16

approprier, s' (ref)	appropriate 7
approuver (tr)	approve 7
appuyer (tr)	lean (thing) against 12
appuyer sur (intr)	depress, press 12
arbitrer (tr)	arbitrate, referee (sport) 7
argenter (tr)	silver, silver-plate 7
armer de courage, s' (ref)	steel oneself 7
armer de, s' (ref)	arm 7
arranger (tr)	arrange, put in order 13
arrêter (tr)	stop, stem, arrest 7
arrêter quelque temps, s' (ref)	to stop over (during flight) 7
arrêter, s' (ref)	stop, draw up (vehicle) 7
arriver (intr)	arrive, happen 7*
arriver à (intr)	get to 7*
arrondir (tr)	round up 16
arroser (tr)	water 7
asperger (tr)	sprinkle 13
aspirer à (intr)	aspire to 7
assaillir (tr)	assail 18
assaisonner (tr)	season, flavour 7
assassiner (tr)	murder, assassinate 7
assembler (tr)	put together 7
assembler, s' (ref)	assemble, flock together 7
asseoir, s' (ref)	sit down, be seated 51 $\boxed{\text{M}}$
assiéger (tr)	besiege 11, 13
assigner (tr)	assign 7
assimiler (tr)	assimilate 7
assister à (intr)	attend, be present at 7
associer (tr)	associate (something) 7
associer, s' (ref)	join with, form an alliance 7
assombrir, s' (ref)	darken 16
assommer (tr)	knock out 7
assortir à, s' (ref)	match 16
assoupir, s' (ref)	drop off, doze 16
assourdir (tr)	deafen 16
assujettir (tr)	steady 16
assurer (tr)	assure, insure, ensure 7
assurer la liaison avec (tr)	liaise with 7
atomiser (tr)	atomize 7
attacher (tr)	attach, fasten, tie up 7
attaquer (tr)	attack 7
atteindre (tr)	attain, arrive at 42
atteler (tr)	harness 9
attendre (tr)	wait, expect 28
attendre avec impatience (tr)	look forward to 28
attendre à, s' (ref)	expect 28

atterrir (intr)	land 16
attirer (tr)	attract, entice 7
attirer, s' (ref)	incur 7
attraper (tr)	catch 7
attrister (tr)	sadden 7
auditionner (tr)	audition 7
augmenter (tr)	increase, raise, add to 7
automatiser (tr)	automate 7
autoriser (tr)	authorize, entitle 7
avaler (tr)	swallow 7
avancer (intr)	be fast/slow 14
avancer (tr)	advance, further, stick out 14
avancer à toute vapeur (intr)	steam ahead 14
avancer, s' (ref)	advance, move forward 14
aventurer, s' (ref)	venture 7
avérer, s' (ref)	turn out 11
avertir (tr)	warn 16
aveugler (tr)	blind 7
avoir (tr)	have, have got 4 M
il y a (tr)	*there is, are*
qu'est-ce qu'il y a? (tr)	*what's the matter?*
il m'a eu (tr)	*he tricked me, took me in*
avoir besoin de (tr)	need 4
avoir chaud (tr)	be hot, feel hot 4
avoir des rapports avec (tr)	relate to 4
avoir des rapports (sexuels) avec (tr)	have intercourse 4
avoir faim (tr)	be hungry 4
avoir froid (tr)	be cold, feel cold 4
avoir honte (tr)	be ashamed 4
avoir la diarrhée (tr)	have diarrhea 4
avoir l'air (intelligent) (tr)	look (intelligent) 4
avoir le mal de mer (tr)	be seasick 4
avoir lieu (tr)	take place 4
avoir l'intention de (tr)	intend 4
avoir l'intention de faire (tr)	intend to 4
avoir mal au coeur (tr)	feel sick 4
avoir peur (tr)	be afraid 4
avoir raison (tr)	be right 4
avoir sept ans (tr)	to be seven years old 4
avoir soif (tr)	be thirsty 4
avoir sommeil (tr)	be sleepy 4
avoir tendance à (tr)	tend 4
avoir tort (tr)	be wrong 4
avoir un accident (tr)	have an accident 4
avoir un compte à (tr)	bank with, at 4

avoir un point de vue (tr)   have a point of view, stand 4
avouer (tr)   admit, confess 7

B   **bagarrer se** (ref)   brawl 7
baigner (se) (tr & ref)   bathe 7
bâiller (intr)   yawn, gape 7
bâillonner (tr)   gag, stifle 7
baiser (tr)   screw (have sex) 7
baisser (tr)   lower, come down 7
baisser se (ref)   stoop 7
balader se (ref)   stroll 7
balancer (tr)   swing 14
balancer se (ref)   rock 14
balayer (tr)   sweep 15
bander (tr)   bandage 7
bannir (tr)   banish 16
baptiser (tr)   baptise 7
barrer (tr)   cancel out, cross out 7
barrer la porte (tr)   bar 7
barricader (tr)   barricade 7
baser sur (intr)   base on 7
battre (tr)   beat, thresh 39
battre du tambour (intr)   beat the drum 39
bavarder (intr)   gossip, chat 7
baver (intr)   dribble 7
bégayer (tr & intr)   stammer 15
bêler (intr)   bleat 7
bénir (tr)   bless 16
bétonner (tr)   concrete over 7
beugler (intr)   bellow 7
bifurquer (intr)   branch off, fork (road) 7
bio-dégrader (intr)   bi-degrade 7
blanchir (tr)   bleach 16
blesser (tr)   wound, offend 7
blesser, se (ref)   hurt oneself 7
bloquer (tr)   block 7
blottir se (ref)   huddle 16
bluffer (intr)   bluff 7
boire (tr)   drink 29   M
boire à petits coups (tr)   sip 29
boiter (intr)   limp 7
bombarder (tr)   bomb, shell 7
bomber (intr)   bulge 7
bondir (intr)   spring 16
border (tr)   border 7

boucher (tr)	cork, plug 7
bouder (intr)	sulk 7
bouger (tr & intr)	move, shift 13
bouillir (intr)	boil 16
bouillonner (intr)	bubble 7
bourdonner (intr)	buzz, hum 7
bourrer (tr)	stuff 7
bourrer de (tr)	cram with 7
bousculer se (tr & ref)	jostle 7
boutonner (tr)	button 7
boxer (intr)	box 7
boycotter (tr)	boycott 7
braconner (intr)	poach (game) 7
braiser (tr)	braise 7
brancher (tr)	connect up to 7
brasser (tr)	brew 7
bricoler (intr)	do it yourself 7
brider (tr)	bridle 7
briller (intr)	shine 7
broder (tr)	embroider 7
broncher (intr)	flinch 7
bronzer se (ref)	tan 7
brosser (tr)	brush 7
brouiller (tr)	blur 7
brouiller se (ref)	fall out, quarrel 7
brouter (tr)	graze 7
broyer (tr)	grind, crush 12
brûler (tr)	burn 7
brûler légèrement (tr)	scorch 7

C

cabrer se (ref)	rear up 7
cacher (tr)	hide, conceal 7
cajoler (tr)	coax 7
calculer (tr)	calculate, compute 7
caler (tr & intr)	wedge, stall 7
câliner (tr)	cuddle, pet 7
calmer (tr)	calm 7
calmer se (ref)	calm down 7
calomnier (tr)	slander 7
cambrioler (tr)	burgle 7
camper (intr)	camp 7
canaliser (tr)	channel 7
capituler (intr)	capitulate 7
capturer (tr)	capture 7
caractériser (tr)	characterize 7

cligner des yeux (intr)	wink, blink 7
cloisonner (tr)	partition off 7
clôturer (tr)	fence 7
clouer (tr)	nail down 7
coasser (intr)	croak 7
cocher (tr)	tick (on list) 7
coexister (intr)	coexist 7
cogner contre (intr)	knock against 7
cohabiter (intr)	cohabit 7
coincider (intr)	coincide 7
collaborer (intr)	collaborate 7
collectionner (tr)	collect 7
coller (tr)	stick, glue 7
colorier (tr)	color in 7
combattre (tr)	fight 39
combiner (tr)	combine 7
commander (tr)	order meal etc 7
commémorer (tr)	commemorate 7
commencer (tr)	begin, start, make a start 14
commettre (tr)	commit 39
communier (intr)	receive communion 7
communiquer (tr)	communicate 7
comparaître (intr)	appear (in court) 32
comparer (tr)	compare 7
compiler (tr)	compile 7
compléter (tr)	complete 11
complimenter (tr)	compliment 7
compliquer (tr)	complicate 7
comploter (tr)	plot 7
comporter se (tr)	behave 7
composer (tr)	compose 7
comprendre (tr)	understand, comprehend 44
comprimer (tr)	compress 7
compromettre (tr)	compromise 39
compter (tr)	count 7
compter sur (intr)	count on, depend on 7
concéder (tr)	concede 11
concentrer (tr)	concentrate 7
concerner (tr)	concern 7
concevoir (tr)	conceive, design 57
conclure (tr)	conclude, close 30 [M]
concourir (tr)	compete, work together 19
condamner (tr)	damn, condemn, blame 7
condamner à une amende (tr)	fine 7
condenser (tr)	condense 7
conduire (tr)	drive, conduct 31 [M]

coordonner (tr)	coordinate 7
copier (tr)	copy 7
corder (tr)	string 7
correspondre (intr)	correspond, write 28
correspondre à (intr)	correspond to 28
corriger (tr)	correct 13
corroder (tr)	corrode 7
corrompre (tr)	corrupt 28
coucher se (ref)	lie down 7
coudre (tr)	sew, stitch 33 M
couler (tr)	sink 7
couper (tr)	cut, clip 7
couper à travers (intr)	cut across 7
couper la gorge à qqn (tr)	cut throat 7
couper ras les cheveux (tr)	crop (hair) 7
courber (tr)	curve, bend 7
courir (intr)	run, race 19 M
couronner (tr)	crown 7
court-circuiter (tr)	short-circuit 7
coûter (tr)	cost 7
couver (tr)	hatch 7
couvrir (tr)	cover 24
couvrir d'ampoules, se (ref)	blister 24
couvrir de nuages, se (ref)	cloud over 24
couvrir (d'un toit) (tr)	roof 24
cracher (tr)	spit 7
crachiner (intr)	drizzle 7
craindre (tr)	fear 42
créditer (tr)	credit 7
créer (tr)	create 7
crépiter (intr)	crackle 7
creuser (tr)	dig, sink (well), hollow out 7
crever (tr)	burst 10
cribler de (tr)	riddle with 10
crier (tr)	shout, cry out 7
cristalliser, se (ref)	crystalize 7
critiquer (tr)	criticize, censure 7
croire (tr)	believe, think 34 M
je ne crois pas (intr)	*I don't think so*
croire en (intr)	believe in 34
crucifier (tr)	crucify 7
cuber (tr)	cube 7
cueillir (tr)	gather, pick 18 M
cuire (tr)	cook 31

**cuire à la vapeur/
à feu doux** (tr) — steam, simmer 31
cuisiner (tr) — cook 7
cultiver (tr) — cultivate, grow, farm 7

D   **daigner** (tr) — deign to 7
danser (intr & ref) — dance 7
dater de (intr) — date back to 7
débarquer (tr & intr) — disembark 7
débarrasser (tr) — clear 7
débarrasser de, se (ref) — dispose of, get rid of 7
débattre (tr) — debate 39
débiter qqn d'une somme (tr) — debit 7
déblayer (tr) — clear away,
remove (obstacle) 15

déborder (tr & intr) — overflow 7
déboucher (tr) — unblock 7
débourser (tr) — pay out 7
déboutonner (tr) — unbutton 7
débrancher (tr) — disconnect 7
débrouiller, se (ref) — cope (with) 7
décerner (tr) — award 7
décevoir (tr) — disappoint 57
décharger (tr) — discharge 13
déchirer (tr) — tear 7
déchirer, se (ref) — rip, tear, be pulled (muscle)
7

décider (tr) — decide 7
décider, se (ref) — make up one's mind 7
décider pour, se (ref) — decide on 7
déclarer (tr) — declare 7
déclarer coupable (tr) — convict 7
déclencher (tr) — trigger off 7
décoder (tr) — decode 7
décoller (intr & tr) — take off (plane); unstick 7
décomposer, se (ref) — decompose 7
décorer (tr) — decorate 7
découper (tr) — cut up 7
découpler (tr) — uncouple 7
décourager (tr) — discourage 13
découvrir (tr) — uncover, discover 24
décréter (tr) — decree 11
décrire (tr) — describe 36
décrocher (tr) — lift phone receiver 7
dédier (tr) — dedicate 7

dédommager pour (tr)	compensate for 13
déduire (tr)	deduce, deduct 31
défaillir (tr)	faint, falter 18
défaire (tr)	undo, untie, unpack 37
défendre (tr)	defend, forbid 28
défier (tr)	challenge 7
défiler (intr)	march past, parade 7
définir (tr)	define 16
déformer (tr)	distort, deform 7
dégeler (tr & intr)	thaw 10
dégivrer (tr)	de-ice, defrost (refrigerator) 7
dégonfler (tr)	deflate 7
dégoûter (tr)	disgust 7
dégoutter (intr)	trickle 7
dégrader (tr)	degrade, deface 7
déguiser (se) (tr & ref)	disguise 7
déjeuner (intr)	have dinner, lunch 7
délayer (tr)	blend, mix 15
déléguer (tr)	delegate 11
délibérer (de) (intr & intr)	deliberate 11
demander (tr)	ask, enquire, request 7
ça demande beaucoup de temps (tr)	*that takes up a lot of time*
demander à qqn de faire	ask (someone to do sth) 7
demander des nouvelles (tr)	ask after 7
demander, se (ref)	wonder 7
démanger (intr)	itch 13
démaquiller, se (ref)	remove make-up 7
démarrer (tr & intr)	start 7
démêler (tr)	disentangle 7
déménager (intr)	move house 7
démissionner (intr)	resign 7
démolir (tr)	demolish 16
démonter (tr)	take down, dismantle 7
démontrer (tr)	how, demonstrate 7
dénigrer (tr)	disparage 7
dénoncer (tr)	denounce 14
dénoter (tr)	denote 7
dénoyauter (tr)	stone 7
dépasser (tr)	surpass, overtake 7
dépêcher, se (ref)	hurry 7
dépéchez-vous! (ref)	*hurry up!*
dépeindre (tr)	depict 42
dépenser (tr)	spend 7
déplacer (tr)	displace 14

déplaire (tr)	displease 43
déposer (tr)	deposit, dump 7
dépouiller (tr)	strip 7
déprécier (intr)	depreciate 7
déprimer (tr)	depress 7
déraisonner (intr)	rave 7
déranger (tr)	disturb 13
déraper (intr)	skid 7
dériver de (intr)	be derived from 7
dérober, se (ref)	back down7
désaltérer, se (ref)	quench 11
désamorcer (tr)	defuse 14
désapprouver (tr)	disapprove 7
désarmer (tr)	disarm 7
désavouer (tr)	disclaim 7
descendre (intr)	come down 8*
descendre (tr)	bring down, carry down 8
le gangster l'a descendu (tr)	*the gangster shot him dead*
désenivrer (tr & intr)	sober up 7
déserter (tr)	desert 7
désespérer, se (ref)	despair 11
déshabiller (tr)	undress (someone) 7
déshabiller, se (ref)	get undressed 7
désherber (tr)	weed 7
déshériter (tr)	disinherit 7
désinfecter (tr)	disinfect 7
désintégrer, se (ref)	disintegrate 11
désirer (tr)	desire 7
désorganiser (tr)	disorganise 7
desservir (tr)	clear away, clear table 25
dessiner (tr)	draw 7
détacher (tr)	detach 7
détacher sur le fond, se (ref)	stand out against 7
détailler (tr)	detail 7
détendre, se (ref)	relax 28
détériorer (intr)	deteriorate 7
détériorer, se (ref)	worsen 7
déterminer (tr)	determine 7
déterminer la quantité de (tr)	quantify 7
déterrer (tr)	dig up 7
détester (tr)	hate 7
détourner (tr)	divert 7
détourner un avion (tr)	hijack 7
détruire (tr)	destroy 31
dévaliser (tr)	rob 7

dévaluer (tr)	devalue 7
dévaster (tr)	devastate 7
développer (tr)	expand 7
devenir (intr)	become 8*
devenir adulte (intr)	grow up 8*
dévier (tr & intr)	deviate 7
deviner (tr)	guess 7
dévisager (tr)	stare at 13
dévisser (tr)	unscrew 7
dévisser se (ref)	come unscrewed 7
devoir (tr)	owe 52 M
devoir (tr)	have to, must 52
devoir quitter (tr)	be called away 52
dévorer (tr)	devour 7
diagnostiquer (tr)	diagnose 7
dicter (tr)	dictate 7
différencier (tr)	differentiate 7
différer (intr)	differ 11
différer de (intr)	be different 11
digérer (tr)	digest 11
diluer (tr)	dilute 7
diminuer (intr)	diminish, lessen 7
dîner (intr)	dine 7
dire (tr)	say, tell 35 M
dire au revoir (tr)	say goodbye, see off 35
dire du mal de (tr)	speak ill of 35
dire merci (tr)	say thank you 35
dire, se (ref)	call, be said 35
cela se dit comment	*how do you say*
en français?	*that in French?*
diriger (tr)	direct 13
diriger un orchestre (tr)	conduct orchestra 13
diriger vers, se (ref)	make for 13
discerner (tr)	discern 7
discipliner (tr)	discipline 7
disculper (tr)	exonerate 7
discuter (intr)	debate 7
discuter de (intr)	discuss 7
disloquer (tr)	disperse 7
disputer, se (ref)	quarrel, argue 7
dissiper, se (ref)	wear off 7
dissoudre (tr)	dissolve 45
dissoudre, se (ref)	dissolve, be dissolved 45
dissuader (tr)	dissuade 7
distiller (tr)	distil 7
distinguer (tr)	distinguish, tell apart 7

distraire (tr)	distract 48
distribuer (tr)	distribute, deal (cards) 7
diverger (de) (intr)	diverge (from) 13
diversifier (tr)	diversify, vary 7
divertir (tr)	entertain 16
diviser (tr)	divide 7
diviser en deux (tr)	halve 7
divorcer (tr)	divorce 14
divorcer, se (ref)	get divorced 14
divulguer (tr)	disclose 7
donner (tr)	give 7
donner à boire à (tr)	water (animals) 7
donner à manger à (tr)	feed (animals) 7
donner de la peine pour, se (tr)	take trouble 7
donner des prévisions météo (tr)	forecast 7
donner pouvoir à (tr)	commission 7
donner sur (intr)	open onto, look out on 7
donner un bain à qqn (tr)	bath 7
donner un coup de pied (tr)	kick 7
donner un coup de poing (tr)	punch 7
donner un coup d'oeil (tr)	glance 7
donner une claque (tr)	smack 7
doper (tr)	dope 7
dormir (intr)	sleep 20 [M]
dormir trop longtemps (intr)	oversleep 20
doubler (tr)	double 7
doucher, se (ref)	shower 7
douter (tr)	doubt 7
drainer (tr)	drain 7
dresser (tr)	pitch 7
dresser une embuscade à (tr)	lie in wait for 7
dresser, se (ref)	stand up, sit up 7
droguer (tr)	drug 7
droguer, se (ref)	take drugs 7
durcir (tr)	harden 16
durer (intr)	last, endure, go on 7

E

éblouir (tr)	dazzle 16
ébrécher (tr)	chip 11
écarter de, s' (ref)	get out of way of 7
échanger (tr)	exchange 13
échapper à (intr)	slip 7
échapper de, s' (ref)	escape from 7
échauffer, s' (ref)	warm up (for sport) 7

échelonner (tr)	stagger, space out 7
échouer à (intr)	fail 7
éclabousser (tr)	splash, spatter 7
éclaircir, s' (ref)	brighten up, clear up (weather) 16
économiser (tr)	economize 7
écorcher (tr)	skin 7
écosser (tr)	shell 7
écouter (tr)	listen 7
écraser (tr)	crush 7
écraser, s' (ref)	crash 7
écrire (tr)	write 36 [M]
écrire pour une demande (tr)	write away 36
écrouler, s' (ref)	subside, collapse 7
éditer (tr)	edit 7
effacer (tr)	rub out 14
effleurer (tr)	brush against 7
effondrer, s' (ref)	flop down 7
effrayer (tr)	scare 15
égaliser (tr)	equalize 7
égaliser, s' (ref)	even out 7
égarer, s' (ref)	stray, wander 7
on s'est égaré (ref)	*we got lost*
égoutter, s' (ref)	drip 7
élaborer (tr)	think out, work out (plan) 7
élargir (tr)	widen, broaden 16
électrifier (tr)	electrify 7
élever (tr)	rear 10
élever à la puissance x (tr)	raise to the power 10
élever à, s' (ref)	amount to, add up to 10
élever une objection contre (tr)	object 10
éliminer (tr)	eliminate 7
élire (tr)	elect 38
éloigner (tr)	move sth away from 7
éloigner, s' (ref)	walk away, move away 7
emballer (tr)	package 7
embarquer (tr & intr)	embark 7
embarrasser (tr)	embarrass 7
embaucher (tr)	engage, employ 7
embellir (tr)	embellish 16
embêter (tr)	annoy 7
embrasser (tr)	embrace, kiss 7
embrumer, s' (ref)	become misty 7
émerger (intr)	emerge from 13
émettre (tr)	emit, send out 39
émigrer (intr)	emigrate 7

emmitoufler, s' (ref)	wrap up 7
émouvoir (tr)	disturb, upset, move 56
empaqueter (tr)	bundle up 7
empêcher (tr)	prevent, hinder 7
empêcher de s'approcher (tr)	keep away 7
empêcher de sortir (tr)	keep in 7
empiffrer, s' (ref)	guzzle 7
empiler (tr)	pile 7
empirer (tr)	worsen, make worse 7
empirer (intr)	get worse, worsen 7
employer (tr)	employ, use 12 [M]
empoigner (tr)	grip, grab 7
empoisonner (tr)	poison 7
emporter (tr)	carry off, take away 7
emprisonner (tr)	imprison 7
emprunter (tr)	borrow 7
émulsifier (tr)	emulsify 7
encadrer (tr)	frame 7
encaisser (tr)	cash 7
encastrer (tr)	box in, build in 7
encercler (tr)	encircle 7
enchaîner (tr)	chain 7
enchanter (tr)	delight 7
encourager (tr)	encourage 13
endommager (tr)	damage 13
endormir, s' (ref)	go to sleep, fall asleep 20
endosser (tr)	endorse 7
enfermer qqn dans (tr)	confine to 7
enfiler (tr)	thread (needle), string (beads) 7
enflammer (tr)	inflame with 7
enflammer, s' (ref)	flare 7
enfoncer (tr)	drive in 14
enfreindre (tr)	contravene 42
enfuir, s' (ref)	flee 22
engager (tr)	hire, involve in 13
engager, s' (ref)	commit oneself 13
engloutir (tr)	gobble 16
engraisser (tr)	fatten 7
enivrer, s' (ref)	get drunk 7
enlever (tr)	take off (shoes, clothes) 10
enlever la coquille (tr)	shell 10
ennuyer (tr)	bore 12
ennuyer, s' (ref)	be bored, get bored 12
enrayer (tr)	curb, check 15
enregistrer (tr)	record 7

enregistrer sur magnétoscope (tr) video, record on video 7
enrhumer, s' (ref) catch cold 7
enrichir (tr) enrich 16
enrouler (tr) coil 7
enseigner (tr) teach 7
entasser (tr) heap 7
entasser, s' (ref) pile up 7
entendre (tr) hear, find out 28
entendre, s' (ref) get along with 28
entendre bien avec, s' (ref) get on well with 28
enterrer (tr) bury 7
entortiller (tr) twist 7
entourer (tr) surround 7
entourer d'une haie (tr) hedge 7
entraîner (tr) train 7
entreprendre (tr) undertake 46
entrer (intr) go in, enter 7*
entrer comme une flèche (intr) shoot in 7*
entrer dans une maison (intr) join firm (business) 7*
entrer en éruption (intr) burst in 7*
entrer en scène (intr) come on (to stage) 7*
entrer rapidement (intr) sweep in 7*
entrer par effraction (intr) break in 7*
entrer dans l'armée (intr) join up 7*
entretenir (tr) maintain, service,
        provide for 26
entretenir avec qqn, s' (ref) confer, converse with 26
entrouvrir (tr) half open 24
envier (tr) envy 7
envoler, s' (ref) fly away 7
envoyer (tr) send 12
envoyer chercher (tr) send for, summon 12
envoyer la facture (tr) bill 12
envoyer par téléfax (tr) fax 12
envoyer (des suggestions) (tr) write in 12
épaissir (tr) thicken 16
épanouir, s' (ref) open out 16
épargner (tr) spare 7
éparpiller (tr) scatter 7
épeler (tr) spell 9
épier (tr) spy on 7
épingler (tr) pin 7
épousseter (tr) dust 9
éprouver (tr) experience 7
épuiser (tr) exhaust 7
équilibrer (tr) balance 7

ça m'est égal (intr)	*I don't care* 5
être en chômage (intr)	be unemployed 5
être en colère (intr)	be angry 5
être en expansion (intr)	boom 5
être en retard (intr)	be late 5
être en séance (intr)	sit, be in session (court, parliament) 5
être la vedette (intr)	star 5
être mannequin (intr)	model 5
être naufragé (intr)	be shipwrecked 5
être nécessaire (intr)	be necessary 5
être obligé de (intr)	be obliged to 5
être parent de (intr)	be related 5
être patient/impatient (intr)	be patient/impatient 5
être permis (intr)	be allowed 5
être pour (intr)	be for 5
être pris de vertiges (intr)	feel dizzy 5
être prudent (intr)	be careful 5
en être quitte pour (intr)	get away with 5
être reçu (intr)	pass (exam) 5
être responsable de (intr)	be liable for 5
être retardé (intr)	be delayed 5
être retenu (intr)	be delayed 5
être sage (intr)	behave 5
être servi de (intr)	be served by 5
être sur le point de (intr)	be about to 5
être très impoli envers qqn (intr)	be rude to 5
être valable (intr)	be valid 5
étudier (tr)	study 7
évacuer (tr)	evacuate 7
évaluer (tr)	appraise 7
évanouir, s' (ref)	faint 16
évaporer s' (ref)	evaporate, boil dry 7
éveiller (tr)	arouse 7
éviter (tr)	avoid 7
éviter de payer (tr)	dodge paying 7
évoluer (intr)	evolve 7
évoquer (tr)	evoke 7
exagérer (tr)	exaggerate 11
examiner (tr)	examine, inspect, check 7
exaspérer (tr)	exasperate 11
excéder (tr)	exceed 11
excéder la limitation de vitesse (tr)	speed 11
excepter (tr)	except 7

faire attention à qch (tr)	mind, watch out for 37
faire bouillir (tr)	boil 37
faire breveter (tr)	patent 37
faire cadeau de (tr)	give away 37
faire chanter (tr)	blackmail 37
faire chauffer (tr)	heat 37
faire cuire (au four) (tr)	bake 37
faire de la gymnastique (tr)	do gymnastics 37
faire de la peine à qqn	upset, distress somebody 37
faire de la publicité (pour) (tr)	advertise 37
faire de la voile (tr)	go sailing 37
faire de l'escrime (tr)	fence (sport) 37
faire de petits travaux (tr)	do odd jobs 37
faire défiler (tr)	scroll (computer) 37
faire demi-tour (tr)	turn back 37
faire des affaires avec (tr)	do business with 37
faire des courses (tr)	shop, go shopping 37
faire des progrès (tr)	progress, make progress 37
faire des recherches (tr)	research 37
faire des signes (tr)	signal 37
faire désintoxiquer, se (ref)	dry out, come off drugs 37
faire don de (tr)	donate 37
faire du bien à (tr)	benefit 37
faire du bruit (tr)	rattle 37
faire du jogging (tr)	jog 37
faire du mal à (tr)	hurt, harm 37
faire du ski (tr)	ski, go skiing 37
faire du stop (tr)	hitch-hike 37
il fait du vent (tr)	*it's windy* (weather)
faire égoutter (tr)	strain 37
faire entrer (tr)	show in, let in 37
faire équipe avec (tr)	team up 37
faire exploser (tr)	set off 37
faire faux bond (tr)	let down 37
faire fonctionner (tr)	operate machine 37
faire frire (tr)	fry 37
il fait froid (intr)	*it's cold* (weather)
faire grâce à (intr)	let off 37
faire grève (intr)	strike 37
faire irruption (intr)	burst in 37
faire jour, se (ref)	dawn 37
faire la cour à (tr)	court 37
faire la culbute (tr)	somersault 37
faire la fête (tr)	have a party, rave 37

faire tort à (tr)	wrong 37
faire un collage (tr)	cut and paste 37
faire un don à (tr)	give charity 37
faire un effort (tr)	make an effort 37
faire un métier (tr)	do 37
faire un pas (tr)	step 37
faire un zoom (tr)	zoom 37
faire une balade (tr)	go for a walk 37
faire une demande (tr)	apply (for job) 37
f**aire une enquête** (tr)	carry out an enquiry 37
faire une entorse, se (ref)	sprain 37
faire une fausse couche (tr)	miscarry 37
faire une mise en plis (tr)	set hair 37
faire une offre de (tr)	bid 37
faire une ordonnance (tr)	prescribe (medicine) 37
faire une pause (tr)	pause 37
faire une promenade (tr)	walk, go for a walk 37
faire une radio de (tr)	X-ray 37
faire une randonnée (tr)	ramble 37
faire une remise de (tr)	discount 37
faire une valise (tr)	pack 37
faire voir, se (ref)	show up 37
falloir (tr)	to be necessary 53 [M]
il ne faut pas fumer	*you must not smoke*
faner (intr)	fade 7
fasciner (tr)	fascinate 7
fatiguer (tr)	tire 7
faufiler, se (ref)	slip 7
favoriser (tr)	favor 7
fêler (tr)	crack 7
féliciter (tr)	congratulate 7
fendre (tr)	split 28
fermenter (tr & intr)	ferment 7
fermer (tr)	close, shut 7
fermer à clef (tr)	lock 7
fermer à double tour (tr)	double lock 7
fermer au verrou (tr)	bolt down 7
fermer avec une	
fermeture éclair (tr)	zip 7
fermer définitivement (tr)	close down 7
ferrer (tr)	shoe (horse) 7
fêter (tr)	feast, celebrate 7
feuilleter (tr)	browse, leaf through 9
fiancer, se (ref)	get engaged 14
fier à, se (ref)	trust 7
filer (tr)	spin 7

filer (intr)	clear off 7
filmer (tr)	shoot 7
filtrer (tr)	filter 7
financer (tr)	finance 14
finir (tr)	finish, end, wind up 16 [M]
finir de travailler (intr)	stop working 16
fixer (tr)	fix 7
fixer le prix (tr)	price 7
flairer (tr)	scent 7
flamber (intr)	blaze 7
flâner (intr)	loiter 7
flatter (tr)	flatter 7
fleurir (intr)	flower 16
flirter (intr)	flirt 7
flotter (intr)	float 7
fonctionner (intr)	work, function 7
fonder (tr)	found 7
fondre (tr)	melt 28
forcer (tr)	force 14
formater (tr)	format 7
former (tr)	form 7
fouetter (tr)	whip 7
fouiller (tr)	search 7
fournir (tr)	supply 16
fracturer (tr)	fracture 7
franchir (tr)	clear, get over (barrier), shoot rapids 16
frapper (tr)	strike 7
frauder (tr)	defraud 7
frayer un passage, se (ref)	force one's way 15
freiner (intr)	brake 7
frémir (intr)	quiver 16
fréquenter (tr)	frequent (place), date (girl/young man) 7
friser (tr)	curl 7
frissonner (intr)	shiver 7
froisser (tr)	crumple, ruffle 7
frotter (tr)	rub 7
frotter au papier de verre (tr)	sandpaper 7
frustrer (tr)	frustrate 7
fuir (tr)	flee 22 [M]
fuire (intr)	leak 31
fumer (intr)	steam, smoke 7
fumer (tr)	smoke (cigarettes etc) 7
fusionner (tr)	merge 7

G

gâcher (tr)	make a mess of 7
gagner (tr)	earn 7
garantir (tr)	guarantee 16
garder (tr)	guard 7
garer (tr)	garage 7
gaspiller (tr)	waste 7
gâter (tr)	spoil 7
gaver, se (ref)	stuff 7
gazouiller (intr)	twitter 7
geler (intr)	freeze 10
gémir (intr)	moan 16
gêner (tr)	trouble, embarass 7
générer	generate 11
gérer (tr)	manage 11
germer (intr)	sprout 7
gifler (tr)	slap 7
glacer (tr)	ice 14
glisser (intr)	slide 7
gonfler (tr)	inflate 7
gonfler, se (ref)	swell 7
goûter (tr)	taste 7
gouverner (tr)	govern, steer 7
graisser (tr)	grease 7
grandir (intr)	grow 16
gratter (tr)	scrape 7
graver (tr)	engrave 7
greffer sur (tr)	graft onto 7
grêler (intr)	hail 7
griffer (tr)	scratch 7
griffonner (tr)	scribble 7
grignoter (tr)	nibble 7
griller (tr)	grill 7
grimper (tr & intr)	climb 7
grincer (intr)	creak 14
grisonner (intr)	go gray (hair) 7
grogner (intr)	growl 7
gronder (intr)	rumble 7
grouiller de (intr)	crawl with 7
grouper, se (ref)	band together 7
guérir (tr & intr)	heal, cure 16
guérir, se (ref)	recover, get better 16
guetter (tr)	look out, lie in wait for 7
guider (tr)	guide 7

H

habiller (tr)	clothe 7
habiller, s' (ref)	get dressed 7
habiter (tr & intr)	live 7
habituer (tr)	accustom 7
habituer, s' (à quelque chose) (ref)	get used to 7
***hacher** (tr)	chop 7
***haleter** (intr)	gasp 10
***handicapper** (tr)	handicap 7
***hanter** (tr)	haunt 7
***harceler** (tr)	nag 10
harmoniser (tr)	harmonize 7
***hâter de faire, se** (ref)	make haste to 7
***hausser les épaules** (tr)	shrug 7
***hausser (le prix)** (tr)	put up (price) 7
***hennir** (intr)	neigh 16
hériter (tr)	inherit 7
hésiter (intr)	hesitate 7
***heurter** (tr)	bump into 7
***heurter à** (intr)	bang on, knock at (door) 7
***heurter â , se** (ref)	collide with 7
***hisser** (tr)	hoist 7
humecter (tr)	dampen, moisten 7
humilier (tr)	humiliate 7
***hurler** (intr)	howl 7
hypothéquer (tr)	mortgage 11

I

idéaliser (tr)	idealize 7
identifier (tr)	identify 7
ignorer (tr)	be unaware of 7
illuminer (tr)	illuminate 7
illustrer (tr)	illustrate 7
imaginer (tr)	imagine 7
imiter (tr)	imitate 7
immigrer (intr)	immigrate 7
immuniser (tr)	immunize 7
importer (intr)	matter 7
importuner (tr)	molest 7
impressionner (tr)	impress 7
imprimer (tr)	print 7
incinérer (tr)	cremate 11
inciser (tr)	incise 7
inciter (tr)	stir 7
incliner la tête (tr)	nod 7
incliner, s' (ref)	bend 7

incorporer (tr) incorporate 7
indiquer (tr) point out/to 7
infecter (tr) infect 7
infecter, s' (ref) become infected 7
influencer (tr) influence 14
informer (tr) advise 7
informer sur, s' (ref) enquire, get information 7
ingérer, s' (ref) interfere 11
initier (tr) initiate 7
injecter qch a qqn (tr) inject 7
inonder (tr) flood 7
inquiéter (tr) worry, bother (someone) 11
inquiéter, s' (ref) worry 11
inscrire, s' (à) (ref) register, enrol (in) 36
insérer (tr) insert 11
insister (intr) insist 7
inspirer (tr) inhale 7
installer (tr) sit 7
installer des micros cachés (tr) bug 7
installer, s' (ref) settle down 7
instruire (tr) instruct 31
insulter (tr) insult 7
intégrer (tr) integrate 11
intensifier (tr) intensify 7
intéresser (tr) interest 7
intéresser à, s' (ref) be interested in 7
interjeter appel (tr) appeal 9
interpréter (tr) interpret, read 11
interroger (tr) interrogate 13
interrompre (tr) interrupt, come in 28
interrompre son voyage (tr) stop off 28
intervenir (intr) intervene, take place, occur 24*
interviewer (tr) interview 7
intriguer (intr) scheme 7
introduire (tr) introduce, show in 31
introduire progressivement (tr) phase in, introduce gradually 31
inventer (tr) invent 7
investir (tr) invest 16
inviter (tr) invite 7
ioniser (tr) ionize 7
irriguer (tr) irrigate 7
irriter (tr) irritate 7
isoler de (tr) isolate from 7

J

jardiner (intr)	garden 7
jaunir (intr)	turn yellow 16
jeter (tr)	throw, cast 9
jeter, se (dans) (ref)	flow into 9
jeter un coup d'oeil à (tr)	peep 9
jeter un pont sur (tr)	bridge 9
jeter une bombe (tr)	throw a bomb 9
joindre (tr)	connect 42
joncher (tr)	strew 7
jouer (tr)	gamble, stake 7
jouer (tr & intr)	act 7
jouer au football (intr)	play soccer 7
jouer d'un instrument (intr)	play an instrument 7
jouer un rôle (tr)	play a part 7
juger (tr)	judge 13
jurer (tr)	swear 7
justifier (tr)	justify 7

K

kidnapper (tr)	kidnap 7
klaxonner (intr)	hoot (vehicle horn) 7

L

labourer (tr)	till (soil) 7
lâcher (tr)	let loose 7
laisser (tr)	leave 7
laisser entrer (tr)	admit 7
laisser passer (tr)	let through 7
laisser tomber (tr)	drop 7
laisser tromper, ne pas, se (ref)	see through 7
**laissez-moi finir** (tr)	_let me finish_
lancer (tr)	fling 14
lancer la balle (tr)	bowl 14
languir (intr)	pine 16
larguer les amarres (tr)	cast off 7
larmoyer (intr)	water 12
laver (tr)	wash 7
laver, se (ref)	wash self 3 M
lécher (tr)	lick 11
légaliser (tr)	legalize 7
léguer (qch à qqn) (tr)	leave, bequeath 11
lever (tr)	raise 10
lever, se (ref)	stand up, get up 10
libérer (tr)	set free 11
lier (tr)	bind, tie 7

lier d'amitié, se (ref)	make friends 7
limer (tr)	file 7
limiter (tr)	limit 7
liquéfier (tr)	liquify 7
lire (tr)	read 38 M
lire à haute voix (tr)	read 38
lisser (tr)	smooth 7
livrer (tr)	deliver 7
loger (tr)	house, accommodate 13
loucher (intr)	squint 7
louer (tr)	rent, hire 7
louer à bail (tr)	lease out 7
louer une place (tr)	reserve, book a seat 7
lubrifier (tr)	oil 7
luire (intr)	gleam 31
lutter (intr)	wrestle 7

M

mâcher (tr)	chew 7
magnétiser (tr)	magnetize 7
magnétoscoper (tr)	video 7
maigrir (intr)	get thin 16
maintenir (tr)	maintain 26
maintenir, se (ref)	keep up 26
maîtriser (tr)	master 7
mal interpréter (tr)	misinterpret 11
maltraiter (tr)	mistreat 7
manger (tr)	eat 13 M
manier (tr)	handle 7
manifester (intr)	demonstrate (in protest) 7
manifester avec violence (intr)	riot 7
manquer (intr)	be missing 7
manquer de (intr)	run out of 7
manquer les cours (tr)	play truant 7
maquiller, se (ref)	make up 7
marchander avec qqn (intr)	bargain 7
marcher (intr)	walk, march, work (machines, arrangements) 1 M
marcher à grand pas (intr)	stride 1
marcher à pied (intr)	hike 1
marier (tr)	marry, perform marriage rite 7
marier, se (ref)	get married 7
marquer (tr)	mark 7
marquer un point, un but (tr)	score goal 7

mettre plus fort (tr)	turn up (radio, hifi) 39
mettre pour la première fois (tr)	wear for first time 39
mettre qch par écrit (tr)	put down in writing 39
mettre sur le compte de qqn (tr)	charge 39
mettre un index (tr)	index 39
mettre en banque (tr)	bank 39
miauler (intr)	mew 7
migrer (intr)	migrate 7
mimer (tr)	mime 7
minuter (tr)	time 7
moderniser (tr)	modernize 7
modifier (tr)	modify 7
moisir (intr)	go mouldy 16
moissonner (tr)	reap 7
monopoliser (tr)	monopolize 7
monter (intr)	rise 7*
monter	
(with auxiliary **avoir**) (tr)	take up, carry up 7
monter à cheval (intr)	ride a horse 7*
monter dans (intr)	board 7*
monter d'une classe (intr)	go up (in school) 7*
monter en flèche (intr)	soar 7*
montrer (tr)	show 7
mordre (tr)	bite 28
motiver (tr)	motivate 7
moudre (tr)	mill, grind 40 M
mouiller (tr)	wet 7
mouler (tr)	mold 7
mourir (intr)	die, pass away 23* M
mourir de faim (intr)	starve 23*
mousser (intr)	foam, froth 7
multiplier (tr)	multiply 7
munir qn de qch (tr)	furnish/equip 16
mûrir (intr)	ripen 16
murmurer (tr)	murmur 7

N

nager (intr)	swim 13
naître (intr)	be born 41* M
narrer (tr)	narrate 7
négliger (tr)	neglect 13
negocier (tr)	negotiate 7
neiger (intr)	snow 13
nettoyer (tr)	clear out 12
nettoyer à la brosse (tr)	scrub 12
neutraliser (tr)	neutralize 7

P

pâlir (intr)	turn pale 16
palper (tr)	feel 7
panser (tr)	dress (wound), groom (horse) 7
paraître (intr)	appear 32
paralyser (tr)	paralyze 7
parcourir (tr)	travel across, look through (book) 19
pardonner (à qqn) (tr)	pardon, forgive someone 7
paresser (intr)	idle about 7
parier (tr)	bet 7
parier sur (intr)	back, gamble on 7
parler (tr & intr)	speak, talk 7 [M]
parler franchement (intr)	speak out 7
partager (tr)	share, share out 13
participer à (intr)	take part, join in 7
partir (intr)	depart, set off, leave 25*
la fusée est partie (intr)	*the rocket lifted off*
passer (intr)	pass, drop in/by 7(*)
passer (tr)	pass, hand round 7
passer au crible (tr)	screen 7
passer de mode (intr)	go out of fashion 7(*)
passer de, se (ref)	dispense with, do without 7
passer en contrebande (tr)	smuggle 7
passer en revue (tr)	survey 7
passer l'aspirateur (tr)	vacuum 7
passer par (intr)	go through 7(*)
passer prendre (tr)	call for 7
passer, se (ref)	occur 7
passer de, se (ref)	do without 7
passer un contrat avec qqn (tr)	contract 7
passer voir (tr)	drop in, call in on 7
passer (à côté) (intr)	pass by 7
patauger (intr)	paddle 13
patiner (intr)	skate 7
paver (tr)	pave 7
payer (tr)	pay 15 [M]
payer les arrhes (tr)	pay a deposit 15
pécher (intr)	sin 11
pêcher (tr)	fish for 7
pédaler (intr)	pedal 7
peigner (tr)	comb 7
peindre (tr)	paint 42 [M]
peler (tr)	peel 10
pendre (tr)	hang 28
pénétrer (tr)	penetrate 11

penser (intr)	think 7
penser à (intr)	have an opinion of 7
penser faire (tr)	consider doing 7
percer (tr)	pierce 14
percevoir (tr)	perceive 57
perdre (tr)	lose 28
perdre son temps (tr)	mess about 28
perdre ses poils (tr)	moult 28
perfectionner (tr)	perfect 7
périr (intr)	perish 16
permettre (tr)	permit 39
permettre, se (ref)	afford 39
persister (intr)	keep at 7
persuader	
(qqn de faire qch) (tr)	persuade someone to do something 7
peser (tr)	weigh 10
peser sur (intr)	weigh down 10
pétiller (intr)	fizz 7
photocopier (tr)	photocopy 7
photographier (tr)	photograph 7
picorer (tr & intr)	peck 7
piler (tr)	pound 7
piloter (tr)	pilot 7
pincer (tr)	pinch 14
pique-niquer (intr)	picnic 7
piquer (tr)	sting, jab, stab 7
piquer un somme (tr)	kip 7
pisser (intr)	piss, urinate 7
son nez pisse le sang (tr)	*his nose is pouring with blood*
placer (tr)	place 14 [M]
plaindre (tr)	pity 42
plaindre, se (ref)	complain 42
plaire (à qqn) (intr)	please (someone) 43 [M]
plaisanter (intr)	joke, have a joke 7
planer (intr)	glide 7
planter (tr)	plant 7
plâtrer (tr)	plaster 7
pleurer (intr)	weep, cry 7
pleuvoir (intr)	rain 54 [M]
plier (tr)	fold 7
plisser (tr)	pleat 7
plomber (tr)	fill (tooth) 7
plonger (tr & intr)	plunge 13
poignarder (tr)	stab 7

poinçonner (tr)	punch 7
pointer à la sortie (intr)	clock out 7
pointer à l'arrivée (intr)	clock in 7
poivrer (tr)	pepper 7
polir (tr)	polish, shine 16
polluer (tr)	pollute 7
polycopier (tr)	duplicate 7
pomper (tr)	pump 7
pondre (tr)	lay 28
porter (tr)	wear, carry 7
porter un toast à (tr)	toast (in champagne etc) 7
porter des fruits (tr)	bear fruit 7
poser (tr)	fit 7
poser une question (tr)	ask a question 7
posséder (tr)	possess 11
poster (tr)	post, mail 7
potasser (intr)	study (hard), swot 7
poudrer (tr)	powder 7
pouffer de rire (intr)	giggle 7
pourchasser (tr)	pursue 7
pourrir (intr)	rot 16
poursuivre (tr)	follow up 47
poursuivre en justice (tr)	prosecute 47
pourvoir (de) (tr)	provide (with) 60
pourvoir en personnel (tr)	staff 60
pousser (tr)	shove 7
pousser avec le doigt (tr)	poke 7
pousser des cris (tr)	scream 7
pousser du doigt (tr)	prod, poke 7
pousser un cri (tr)	call out 7
pousser un cri aigu (tr)	squeal 7
pouvoir	can 55 [M]
je peux . . . ?	*may I . . . ?*
pourriez-vous . . .	*could you . . . ?*
on pourrait peut-être . . .	*perhaps we could . . .*
pratiquer (tr)	practise 7
prêcher (tr)	preach 7
précipiter (tr)	precipitate 7
précipiter hors de, se (ref)	burst out 7
précipiter, se (ref)	rush, dash 7
prédire (tr)	predict 35
préférer (tr)	prefer 11
je préférerais (tr)	*I'd prefer*
prendre (tr)	take 44 [M]
prendre au piège (tr)	trap 44
prendre congé (tr)	take leave 44

promouvoir (tr)	promote 56 [M]
prononcer (tr)	pronounce 14
prononcer une condamnation (tr)	sentence 14
proposer (tr)	propose 7
prospérer (intr)	thrive 11
prostituer, se (ref)	prostitute oneself 7
protéger (tr)	protect 11/13
protester (tr)	protest 7
prouver (tr)	prove 7
publier (tr)	issue 7
puer (tr)	stink 7
puiser (tr)	draw (water, resources) 7
pulvériser (tr)	grind 7
punir (tr)	punish 16
purifier (tr)	purify 7

Q

qualifier (tr)	qualify 7
questionner (tr)	question, interrogate 7

R

raccourcir (tr)	shorten 16
raccourcir, se (ref)	become shorter 16
raccrocher (intr)	ring off 7
raconter (tr)	tell, relate (a story) 7
radiodiffuser (tr)	broadcast 7
radoter (intr)	ramble on 7
raffiner (tr)	refine 7
rafraîchir (tr)	freshen 16
raidir (tr)	stiffen 16
raidir, se (ref)	harden, become stiff 16
raisonner (intr)	reason 7
ralentir (tr)	slow down 16
rallier (tr)	rally, unite 7
rallier à, se (ref)	join with, side with 7
rallonger (tr)	draw out, become longer 13
ramasser (tr)	pick up 7
ramasser à la pelle (tr)	scoop up 7
ramer (intr)	row 7
ramollir (tr)	soften 16
ramoner (tr)	sweep 7
ramper (intr)	crawl, creep 7
ranger (tr)	tidy up, put away 13
ranger du côté de, se (ref)	side with, support 13

raper (tr)	grate 7
rapiécer (tr)	patch 14
rappeler (tr)	ring/call back (telephone); remind, recall 9
rappeler, se (ref)	remember 9
rapporter (tr)	bring back, take back 7
rapprocher de, se (ref)	approximate 7
raser (tr)	shave (someone else) 7
raser, se (ref)	shave (oneself) 7
rationner (tr)	ration 7
ratisser (tr)	rake 7
rattraper (tr)	catch up with 7
rayer (tr)	rule, cross out 15
réagir (intr)	react 16
réaliser (tr)	realize, effect 7
rebondir (intr)	bounce 16
rebrousser chemin (tr)	turn back 7
recevoir (tr)	get 57 M
recharger (tr)	charge (electrical) 13
réchauffer (tr)	heat up, warm up 7
réchauffer, se (ref)	get warm, warm up 7
recommander (tr)	recommend 7
récompenser (tr)	reward 7
réconcilier (tr)	reconcile 7
reconnaître (tr)	recognize 32
reconquérir (tr)	reconquer 17
reconstruire (tr)	reconstruct 31
recopier (tr)	write out 7
recoucher (tr)	to put back to bed 7
recourir à (intr)	resort to, have recourse to 9
recouvrer (tr)	recover, regain 7
recouvrir (tr)	cover over, cover again, hide 24
rectifier (tr)	rectify 7
reculer (intr)	reverse, move back 7
recupérer (tr)	salvage get back 11
recycler (tr)	recycle 7
rédiger (tr)	draw up, edit 13
rédiger le compte-rendu (tr)	minute 13
redoubler (tr)	increase, redouble; repeat year at school 7
redouter (tr)	dread 7
redresser (tr)	straighten, set upright 7
redresser, se (ref)	sit up 7
réduire (tr)	reduce, cut down 31

réduire en esclavage (tr)	enslave 31
refaire (tr)	redo 37
refaire qqn de qch (tr)	do out of 37
réfléchir (intr)	reflect 16
réfléchir à (intr)	think over 16
refléter (tr)	reflect (light) 7
réfrigérer (tr)	refrigerate 11
refroidir (tr)	cool down 16
refuser (tr)	turn down 7
réfuter (tr)	refute 7
regarder (tr)	look at, watch 7
regarder fixement (tr)	stare at, gaze at 7
régler (tr)	settle 11
régler sa note (tr)	check out, pay bill 11
régler un compte (tr)	pay 11
regretter (tr)	be sorry 7
rejeter (tr)	reject 9
rejoindre (tr)	rejoin 42
rejoindre, se (ref)	link up 42
réjouir, se (ref)	rejoice 16
relâcher (tr)	loosen, slacken 7
relayer (tr)	relay 15
relever (tr)	lift, heighten 10
remarquer (tr)	remark, notice 7
rembobiner (tr)	rewind, wind back (cassette) 7
rembourser (tr)	reimburse 7
remercier (tr)	thank 7
remettre à (tr)	hand over 39
remettre à plus tard (tr)	postpone 39
remettre à zéro (tr)	boot (computer) 39
remettre au lendemain (tr)	procrastinate 39
remettre en liberté (tr)	release 39
remettre, se (ref)	recover, get better 39
remonter (tr)	wind up (clock) 7
remorquer (tr)	tow 7
remplacer (tr)	replace, stand in for 14
remplir (tr)	fill, fill in 16
remuer (tr)	stir, wag (tail) 7
rencontrer (tr)	meet 7
rencontrer par hasard (tr)	run into 7
rendre (tr)	give back 28
rendre compte de (tr)	account for 28
rendre compte de, se (ref)	realize 28
rendre fou (tr)	madden 28
rendre inapte (tr)	disqualify 28

rester (intr)	stay 7*
rester à jeun (intr)	fast 7*
rester en arrière (intr)	stop behind, drop back 7*
rester là (intr)	stand by 7*
résulter de (intr)	result from 7
résumer (tr)	summarize 7
retarder (tr & intr)	delay, be slow (clock) 7
retenir (tr)	hold back, detain 26
retentir (intr)	blare, echo 16
retirer (tr)	draw out 7
retirer, se (ref)	withdraw 7
retourner (tr)	turn upside down 7
retourner (intr)	return, go back 7*
retourner, se (ref)	turn round 7
rétrécir (tr)	shrink 16
rétrécir, se (ref)	narrow 16
retrouver (tr)	find again, meet 7
retrouver, se (ref)	meet each other (arranged) 7
réunir (tr)	reunite, amalgamate 16
réussir (intr)	succeed, take off (project) 16
réussir à (intr)	succeed in, pass (exam) 16
réussir à faire (tr)	manage to do, succeed in doing 16
revaloir (tr)	pay back, get even 59
rêvasser (intr)	daydream 7
réveiller (tr)	wake (someone) 7
réveiller, se (ref)	wake up 7
révéler, se (ref)	appear, be revealed, turn out 11
revenir (intr)	return 26*
revenir à soi (intr)	come around, recover consciousness 26*
revenir périodiquement (intr)	come around (to see) 26*
rêver (tr & intr)	dream 7
reviser (tr)	review, revise 7
revivre (tr)	revive (someone) 50
révolter contre, se (ref)	revolt against 7
rider (tr)	wrinkle 7
ridiculiser (tr)	ridicule 7
rincer (tr)	rinse 7
rire (intr)	laugh 46 M
risquer (tr)	risk, chance 7
rompre (tr & intr)	break, break off 28

sentir, se (ref)	feel 25
séparer (tr)	separate 7
séparer de (tr)	separate from 7
séparer de, se (ref)	part (company) 7
serrer (tr)	clamp 7
servir (tr)	serve; bowl (sport) 25
servir à boire (tr)	serve drinks 25
servir à (+ infinitive) (intr)	serve to, be used for 25
servir de, se (ref)	use 25
servir de (intr)	to put to use as 25
shooter (intr)	shoot (soccer) 7
shooter, se (ref)	inject oneself with drugs 7
siffler (intr)	hiss, whistle 7
signer (tr)	sign 7
signer, se (ref)	cross oneself 7
signifier (tr)	mean 7
situer, se (ref)	be located 7
soigner (tr)	care for 7
solder (tr)	sell cheap 7
solidifier (tr)	solidify 7
songer (tr & intr)	dream, think 2
sonner (intr)	sound 7
sonner l'heure (tr)	chime 7
sortir (tr)	bring out 25
sortir (intr)	go out 16*
sortir comme un ouragan (intr)	storm out 16*
sortir comme une flèche (intr)	dart out 25*
sortir de (intr)	go out of 25*
soucier de, se (ref)	care about 7
souder (tr)	weld 7
souffler (intr)	blow 7
souffrir (intr)	suffer 24
souffrir de (intr)	suffer from 24
souhaiter (tr)	wish, wish for, long for 7
souhaiter la bienvenue à (tr)	welcome 7
soulager (tr)	relieve 13
soulever (tr)	raise 10
soulever, se (ref)	rise 10
souligner (tr)	underline, emphasize 7
soumettre (tr)	subject 39
soumettre, se (ref)	submit 39
soumettre à, se (ref)	abide by (rules) 39
soupçonner (tr)	suspect 7
soupirer (intr)	sigh 7
soupirer après (intr)	pine for 7
sourire (intr)	smile 46

taire, se (ref)	be silent 43
tambouriner (tr & intr)	drum 7
tamiser (tr)	sieve 7
taper (tr & intr)	hit, beat 7
taper à la machine (tr)	type 7
elle tape 60 mots par minute (tr)	*she types 60 words per minute*
taper du pied (intr)	stamp 7
taper sur les nerfs de qqn (intr)	get on nerves of 7
tapir, se (ref)	cower 16
tapisser les murs (tr)	hang wallpaper 7
tapoter (tr & intr)	tap 7
taquiner (tr)	tease 7
taxer (tr)	tax 7
téléphoner (qch, à qqn) (tr)	telephone 7
témoigner (intr)	witness, testify 7
témoigner de qch (tr)	bear witness to 7
tendre (tr)	tense, hold out 28
tendre une embuscade (tr)	ambush 28
tenir (tr & intr)	hold 26 M
tiens! (intr)	*I say!*
tenir bon (intr)	hold one's own 26
tenir compte de (tr)	take into account, allow for 26
tenir le coup (tr)	bear up 26
tenir, se (ref)	stand 26
tenter (tr)	tempt 7
terminer (tr)	finish off, end 7
terminer en pointe (intr)	taper 7
terrifier (tr)	terrify 7
terroriser (tr)	terrorize 7
tirer (tr)	pull, draw, shoot 7
il a tiré plusieurs coups de feu (tr)	*he fired several shots*
tirer des exemplaires (tr)	duplicate, run off copies 7
tirer sans gains ni pertes, s'en (intr)	break even 7
tisser (tr)	weave 7
tolérer (tr)	tolerate, put up with 11
tomber (intr)	fall 2* M
tomber amoureux (intr)	fall in love 2*
tomber en panne (intr)	break down 2*
tomber malade (intr)	fall ill 2*
tondre (tr)	shear 28
tondre le gazon (tr)	mow the lawn 28

tonner (intr)	thunder 7
tordre (tr)	wring 28
tordre, se (la cheville) (ref)	twist (ankle) 28
torturer (tr)	torture 7
toucher (tr)	touch, press; receive (money) 7
tourner (tr & intr)	turn 7
tousser (intr)	cough 7
tracasser (tr)	worry, play up 7
traduire (tr)	translate 31
trahir (tr)	betray 16
traîner (intr)	linger 7
traire (tr)	milk (cow) 48 M
traiter (tr)	treat 7
traiter le texte (tr)	word-process 7
trancher (tr)	slice 7
transcrire (tr)	transcribe 36
transférer (tr)	transfer, download (IT) 11
transformer (tr)	transform 7
transmettre (tr)	pass down 39
transporter (tr)	transport, ship 7
traquer (tr)	hound 7
travailler (intr)	work 7
travailler au noir (intr)	moonlight 7
travailler bien (intr)	work hard, get on with 7
travailler comme un forcené (intr)	work like mad 7
travailler dur (intr)	work hard 7
traverser (tr)	go across, cross 7
trébucher (intr)	trip, stumble 7
trembler (intr)	tremble 7
tremper (tr)	soak, steep, dip 7
tresser (tr)	twine 7
tricher (intr)	cheat 7
tricoter (tr)	knit 7
trier (tr)	sort 7
tromper (tr)	mislead 7
tromper, se (ref)	be mistaken 7
trouver (tr)	find 7
trouver, se (ref)	be found, be 7
trouver à redire à (tr)	object to 7
tuer (tr)	kill 7
tutoyer (se) (tr & ref)	say 'tu' (address informally) 12
tyranniser (tr)	bully 7

U

unir (tr)	unite 16
unir, s' (ref)	bond 16
uriner (intr)	urinate 7
user (tr)	wear out 7
user, s' (ref)	wear out, become worn out 7
utiliser (tr)	use 7

V

vaciller (intr)	flicker 7
vaincre (tr)	overcome 49 M
valoir (intr)	be worth 59 M
vanter, se (ref)	boast 7
vaporiser (tr)	spray 7
vaporiser, se (ref)	vaporize 7
varier (tr)	vary 7
vendre (tr)	sell, stock, market 28 M
vendre au détail (tr)	retail 28
vénérer (tr)	worship, revere 11
venir (intr)	come 26*
venez vous asseoir auprés de nous	*come and join us*
venir à échéance (intr)	fall due 26*
venir à l'esprit (intr)	occur 26*
venir de Rome (intr)	come from Rome 26*
venir de faire (intr)	have just done 26*
venir voir (tr)	come and see, come round 26*
ventiler (tr)	ventilate 7
vérifier (tr)	verify, check, audit 7
verser (tr)	pour 7
vêtir (tr)	dress (someone) 27 M
vêtir, se (ref)	dress (self) 27
vexer (tr)	spite 7
vibrer (intr)	vibrate 7
vider (tr)	empty 7
vieillir (intr)	get old 16
violer (tr)	rape 7
viser (tr)	aim at 7
visiter (tr)	visit 7
visser (tr)	screw on/down 7
visualiser (tr)	display 7
vivre (intr)	live 50 M
vivre en marge de la société (intr)	drop out 50
voiler (tr)	veil 7